God, Allah, and Ju Ju

BY JACK MENDELSOHN

Why I Am a Unitarian

God, Allah, and Ju Ju

Religion in Africa Today

BY

JACK MENDELSOHN

GREENWOOD PRESS, PUBLISHERS
WESTPORT, CONNECTICUT

Library of Congress Cataloging in Publication Data

Mendelsohn, Jack, 1918-
God, Allah, and Ju Ju.

Reprint of the ed. published by T. Nelson, New York.
Bibliography: p.
Includes index.
1. Africa, Sub-Saharan--Religion. I. Title.
[BR1430.M4 1978] 200'.967 78-5872
ISBN 0-313-20483-7

Reprinted with the permission of Thomas Nelson Inc.

Reprinted in 1978 by Greenwood Press, Inc.,
51 Riverside Avenue, Westport, CT. 06880

Printed in the United States of America

10 9 8 7 6 5 4 3 2 1

TO

THAT SMALL CIRCLE OF MEN AND WOMEN IN EACH AFRICAN SOCIETY, WHO HUNGER FOR WHAT IS ESSENTIALLY AFRICAN, EVEN AS THEY THIRST FOR THE BEST OF THE WORLD'S LEARNING AND MODERNITY. THEY ARE STILL FEW IN NUMBER, AND ARE HAVING NO EASY TIME OF IT.

"The Pot is boiling because somebody makes it boil."

—African proverb

Preface

I ACCEPT African independence without reservations. This is my "bias" and it is well to state it at the beginning. I acknowledge, also without reservations, the equal moral dignity of Africans. I believe that Africans are under no more obligation to "justify" their freedom and dignity than Westerners are. Nor are they under any less obligation. We—Africans and Westerners—are of the same species.

In practical terms the outcome of African freedom will depend on many forces, some of which are purely African. Others, however, are much influenced by Western sentiments, conduct, and relations with Africa.

A good many of these forces are political and economic. They are written about profusely. But politics and economics are not the only forces shaping Africa's future. Religion is also a factor to be reckoned with, a vitally important one. Little enough has been written of it, especially in the broad fashion of this book.

Questions of profound significance for Africa and for the sentiments of Westerners about Africa, are:

What is the future of Christianity as the religious commitment of Africa's rising leadership?

What is the future of Islam in the same context?

What moral base do African elitists see being built under the newly independent societies? What do African intellectuals mean when they appeal to traditional African spiritual values as such a base? If magic is an inherent part of such traditional values, how does it affect moral and intellectual development?

What kind of religious and moral training does the African intelligentsia advocate as part of the educational process?

What does the concept of the separation of church and state mean in modern African society?

How does religious commitment relate to the over-all style of life of African leaders?

What vital relevance is there, if any, in the traditional African structure of *teme*, the unseen, spirit world?

How does all of this relate to the allure of Communism as an alternative spiritual force?

In the torrent of literature about Africa, these questions are often dealt with *separately*, but to my knowledge there has been no effort to bring them together in coherent fashion. This is my justification for entering an already overcrowded field. My book is meant to be provocative rather than exhaustive. It ends with a reading list for those who would like to retrace at least some of the paths of research which I have followed. Not everyone can duplicate the traveling and interviewing I have done in Africa, but all can deepen their knowledge and understanding of Africa's current spiritual dispositions and indispositions. The case for African independence does not rely on the informed opinion of Westerners, but if Westerners are to help Africans make the best use of their freedom, it matters profoundly that there should be keener insight into the issues and problems probed in this book. Africans are entitled to their freedom whether they make good use of it or not. It is ridiculous, however, to leave the matter at that.

For the present, educated men and women with civic spirit and spiritual depth are in painfully short supply in Africa. Their ranks will increase, but right now the spiritual views of a tiny elite are momentous. For this reason I am particularly grateful to Dr. E. U. Essien-Udom, of Nigeria and the Center for International Affairs at Harvard, for his assistance in exploring and reporting the religious feelings of Africa's small circle of intellectuals. In the main, I have let them speak for themselves and have avoided editorial temptations.

I acknowledge also a special debt to Robin Horton, whose studies provided me with invaluable material on the Kalabari people.

This is a book about Africa south of the Sahara. I am well aware that the desert and vast areas north of it exist, and that a book about "African" religion might well have been widened to embrace the entire continent. But the Sahara is more than a geographical divider. It separates culturally as well.

Robertson Smith began his classic study, *Religion of the Semites,* with these words: "No positive religion that has moved man has been able to start with a *tabula rasa,* and express itself as if religion were beginning for the first time; in form, if not in substance, the new system must be in contact all along the line with the older ideas and practices which it finds in possession. A new scheme of faith can find a hearing only by appealing to religious instincts and susceptibilities that already exist . . . , and it cannot reach these without taking account of the traditional forms in which all religious feeling is embodied, and without speaking a language which men accustomed to these old forms can understand."

Here is a spirit with which I ardently agree. Evolution and

synthesis, not conquest, are the keys to religion's future in Africa. For those of us who desire better understanding of what is happening to African souls, it is well to travel with unshod feet; that is, without the prejudices inescapably clamped upon us by our own culture.

In the past, African life has been essentially religious. The individual's relationship to the family, the clan, and the tribe —morality, law, worship, celebration, politics, social status, economics, manners, war and peace—all that was sustaining or weakening in African life, has been anchored in African religion. To say that the Western influences playing upon African life at a thousand points have shattered the old patterns is merely to repeat an axiom that is already dulled by repetition. Yet the fact remains, and the question now is whether African life will continue to be essentially religious. If so, in what forms? If not, with what results?

It has been said that African traditional religion is not so much thought out as danced out. If I were not well encrusted with a shell of Western inhibitions, I would "dance out" in African fashion my thanks to my wife, Ruth, who has shared the labors of this book in most practical ways. There is a Baronga tribal proverb: "Any man who attempts to swallow a large stone certainly has confidence in the size of his throat." In some respects the writing of this book has been an attempt "to swallow a large stone," but my confidence has been in my wife's ability to pull me through. That confidence was not misplaced.

JACK MENDELSOHN.

Boston, Massachusetts

Contents

God, Allah, and Ju Ju

I

Africa's Tarnished Cross

After dinner, around nine o'clock, majestic Ben Nzeribe came for me. It is *Dr.* Ben Nzeribe, the doctorate from Cornell University in Ithaca. This Ph.D. in Agricultural Economics, salaried by the Unitarian Service Committee, Inc. and assisted by its field personnel, is back in his home village of Awo Omamma in eastern Nigeria where he has become a kind of uncrowned high chief. Around him cluster the energies of scores of self-help development projects: schools, roads, latrines, a hospital, nutrition, experimental farming. Awo Omamma is on the move into the twentieth century, and this young man is the catalyst, the spur, the transfusion.

The beat of drums fills the heavy night air. It is the eve of the *Owu,* a period of dancing and feasting which marks the beginning of the yam harvest. Ben has come to escort me to the council hut, where the elders of his kindred are to hold their own private ushering-in party.

The hut—round, open-sided, roofed with a cone of matting —is a hundred yards from the compound. As we walk through the darkness, I try to remember what Ben has told me about the Owu. Yams. As long as they last, the bellies of Awo Omamma are filled with an especially succulent *foo-foo*. The yam meal is kneaded and molded into great mounds of a milky, doughy substance resembling dumplings. Hands reach in, and disengage lumps which are skillfully rolled by the fingers into bite-size balls. These are swished through a pot of steaming, peppery stew, then eaten.

Foo-foo, the staple diet of the Nigerian bush, is made from cassava during the long months after the yams run out. But cassava to yam is like goat to spring lamb. So the coming of the yam harvest is a time of expectancy.

"It is an ancient festival," Ben had said, "but like so many other things around here, people have lost touch with its meaning. Ever since I got back home, I've been warming them up to the idea of the importance of these old rites. It's all part of the psychology of waking them up, and of helping them to feel proud of who they are."

The full meaning of this eludes me, but I recall that Ben had made a subtle connection of his "project revival" with his ill-concealed distaste for missionaries. "We are plagued by Christians," he said. "It isn't just the canards about putting Mother Hubbards on our bare-breasted women; it's the way so many of us were made to feel ashamed of the old customs. This will be the biggest Owu in years. Hundreds of the men are coming back from Lagos, from Enugu, even from the Cameroons."

The hundreds of men Ben referred to were representatives of the thousands of Awo Omamma tribesmen making their way in the cities as tradesmen, stewards, small merchants, government functionaries. Together they fashion the extended network of the Awo Omamma Patriotic Union, the real force behind Nzeribe's village reforms. Awo Omamma is not a "village" by American standards, but more like a county: a loosely knit community of about twenty-five thousand souls spread over many square miles of sandy soil, tangled underbrush, palm-oil trees, and haphazard plantings of yams, cassava, and corn. For the most part, the people have lived for centuries on a subsistence level in isolated mud-hut compounds. In tree-shaded family courtyards, children play in the skin nature provided them, and women dress only from the waist down. But when they come out onto the new web of pounded and graded roads which Nzeribe and his volunteer work crews have hacked out of the bush, the children are generally clothed in shorts purchased from itinerant traders, and the women deck themselves in colorful wrap-arounds.

As many as three or four thousand of Awo Omamma's able-bodied males are, at any given moment, earning their living in some distant city. Among them are elders and skilled dancers and drummers. Without their presence for a festival occasion like the Owu, much of the impact of the rite would be lost.

What Ben Nzeribe had succeeded in doing was to so increase the pride of his absent fellow-villagers in their identity as Awo Omammans that hundreds of them had made the decision to return for the Owu. This was a victory which apparently had to be won over a kind of shamed indifference toward customs labeled "pagan" by mission spokesmen. And obviously one did not lightly dismiss the influence of an Irish Roman Catholic mission which, until just eighteen months before, had been Awo Omamma's sole source of elementary education and rudimentary medical care for expectant mothers.

These are the thoughts filling my mind as Ben and I enter the council hut, where flickering kerosene lamps throw an eerie glow over a circle of ten men sitting upon stools or squatting on the hard dirt floor. One or two of them are in their twenties. One or two, much older. The rest, in between. Their greeting is formal but friendly. I am seated on a stool, with Ben on my right, and a fantastically robed, bulgy-eyed gentleman on my left. Ben tells me in a whisper that he is the story-teller, or "singer," and "the best in all of Ibo land."

A performance has been interrupted by our entrance, but now we are settled, and the story-teller begins again. Never have I heard anything quite like this. He speaks in a piercing, high-pitched voice. Words flow like a torrent—half sung, half spoken. His eyes bulge out even further, until I am certain they will pop onto the kerosene lamps in the circle's center. His listeners are utterly entranced. They hang on every word. Their glistening faces are tauter than bowstrings. Suddenly they burst into laughter. Ben leans over and tells me, "He has just finished a riddle. He asked 'which is worse, a bad child or a bad wife?' Then he answered, 'A man can divorce a bad wife, but a bad child is with him always.' "

I realize this must be a drastically edited version of the riddle, for the story-teller had taken at least five minutes to recount it. Ben is telling me more. "A singer like this one is a highly honored person because he is a professional. It has taken him many years to learn his millions of words, and his genius is that he never changes a single word in retelling his material."

"What do you mean by his *material?*" I ask.

"Literally hundreds upon hundreds of tribal legends, myths, historical events, parables, riddles, and jokes—all kinds of things. He has to be able to tell them in *exactly* the same way each time. If he should ever misplace a syllable, he would be in disgrace."

"How would you know?"

"Maybe we would; maybe we wouldn't. We all know some of the stuff. Anyway, he can't afford to take a chance."

By this time the story-teller is hard at it again, but a new feature has been added to the party. A young man has arrived with two huge casks of palm wine. The singer alternately drones or screams on, and Ben leans over again and informs me we are now hearing some Ibo philosophy about good and evil. Large glass tumblers, meanwhile, are being filled with palm wine. Each man, as he is served, tosses off his libation without pausing for breath. I gingerly sip mine—and nearly lose my supper. To me it smells and tastes like gasoline.

Minutes pass. With a resounding peroration, the storyteller brings his discourse to an end. There is much appreciative murmuring and nodding, and another round of palm wine. This time the singer is included, and he downs two tumblers full in quick succession. Meanwhile, suddenly, one of the men is on his feet and dancing. Ben whispers, "He's not one of our professional dancers. He's just expressing himself."

His dancing looks competent enough to me, but it is plain that the other men are jokingly critical. Two men are now dancing in a kind of challenge round. There is a great deal of laughter.

The indefatigable singer, his thirst momentarily quenched, goes into high gear again. The dancing stops.

For what seems like hours this cycle of events continues. All the while the unusual behavior of one man becomes more and more conspicuous to me. He is not participating as the rest are. Of indeterminate age, perhaps fifty, he wears a limp, grease-stained felt hat, a faded blue shirt, gray cotton trousers, and loose-fitting, tattered sandals. He sits on the ground, slightly outside the circle, with his knees drawn up under his chin, his eyes half-closed.

Suddenly this man is on his feet, dancing around the hut like a dervish. As he shuffles and zigzags in front of the lamps, his shadow lengthens weirdly, and a kind of ecstatic possession seems to come upon him. With wild leaps, he begins to throw his long, thin legs in all directions. About his neck is a tarnished cross on a string, which bobs and spins with the violent motions of his body.

There are roars of approving laughter from the other men. Obviously something terribly exciting and different is taking place. The chief elder of the kindred dashes out of the hut and fires off a thundering blast on an old handmade blunderbuss.

When the uproar subsides, Ben Nzeribe leans toward me, his eyes gleaming. "Do you know what that was all about?" he asks.

"Lord, no," I answer.

"That man is one of our more ardent Christians," Ben says. "Because the missionaries told him not to, he hasn't danced for years. But tonight he danced! He couldn't resist any longer."

It is apparent that every man in the ring shares Ben's glee. A lost brother has been welcomed back into the fold. The "prodigal" himself is no longer just outside the circle. He is very much a part of it. He is winded, but his gaunt, wrinkled face wears a beatific grin. With shaking hands he downs a tumbler of palm wine.

During the days of dancing which followed, I saw this drama repeated many times. Always the theme was the same. Someone whose Christian commitment had kept him from dancing would throw off the restraints and dance, while the others would cheer his "emancipation," his return to Africanism. It was a drama symbolic of significant happenings in Africa's religious life.

A vast spiritual ferment troubles Africa. Christianity, stuck with a colonial label, is in serious trouble. Islam is on the move. Native religious cults and practices, though waning in some sectors, are waxing in others. Ancient festivals, dancing, drumming, and nature rites are looked upon with new interest and excitement, even by educated and sophisticated young Africans, as cultural expressions of the African spirit. The old gods and spirits are in retreat, yet the aspiring African, in his search for self-identity, is on the hunt for religious inspirations which are firmly and unmistakably "African."

What of the Christian missionary movement? Its slow but steady progress has now run headlong into the "new" Africa. The charges leveled against it are both humorous and biting.

In their freewheeling moods, young Africans never seem to tire of retelling the old chestnut:

"The missionaries came to us and said, 'We want to teach you to pray.' 'Good,' we said. 'We would like to learn to pray.' So the missionaries told us to close our eyes. We closed our eyes and learned to pray. When we opened our eyes, there was a Bible in our hands, but our land was gone!"

But there are also the bitter words—words repeated endlessly across the breadth of Africa:

"The Christian missionary movement was an attempt to quench the African spirit. It tried to turn Africans into European Christians. It kicked down our culture to show us which side God was on."

"Missionaries are unrealistic about polygamy."

"Wherever the white man still has the upper hand, the missions remain strangely tolerant of racial discrimination."

"The missionaries drag their feet when it comes to training Africans for church leadership and authority."

"The missions have been indifferent, even hostile, toward African nationalism. There's been no real sympathy for the political aspirations gripping young Africans."

A top figure in the government of Ghana told me: "After much reflection I have decided against having any church connection. Churches are helping very little to solve Ghana's spiritual problems. They seem primarily interested in financial contributions and Sunday morning attendance. Their attitude seems to be that if you take care of these things, God is satisfied. Our young people need something they are not getting, and I can't blame them for not wanting to go to church to hear dogmas the preachers themselves do not really believe."

A man advancing rapidly in Nigerian politics said: "I don't want to appear ungrateful. If it wasn't for Christian mission schools most of us would have had no education. But the churches haven't kept up with the times or with the African spirit. We need something more stimulating than Bible stories and strictures against tribal celebrations and dances."

An Anglican missionary, over a cup of tea in Nairobi, asked plaintively: "Can't you do something about the American fundamentalists? They're over here in force, with lots of money to spend, and for every African they convert, they sour a hundred with their insistence on white domination of the missions and their scorn for politics."

A prosperous Kikuyu farmer pointed toward the top of a hill in the "black highlands" of Kenya: "You see that mission up there. They run an orphanage, a trade school, and a hospital, all for the benefit of us Kikuyus, but do you know that I have never seen a white priest down here at any of our village meetings or rites. If that's Christianity, we can get along without it."

A British professor at University College in Ibadan made this observation: "Many city Africans have only the vaguest notions about the ancient customs of their people. But with nationalism there comes a strong desire to glorify the culture of the past: to create or re-create truly African art forms and spiritual expressions. Christian spokesmen often give the unfortunate impression of being hysterically opposed to this. To the young African of today, it's like opposition to his being an African."

A Bantu Presbyterian minister, at a secret meeting in Johannesburg, said to me, his face contorted with emotion:

"Every day it gets harder and harder to convince my people to keep their Christian faith. They want to know how long they can go on being Christians when Christianity is the religion of the Boer government which treats them as sub-human."

Spicing the nightmares of Christian leaders is the rising crescent of Islam. In most parts of Africa, Moslem conversions are far outstripping Christian gains. Among the rising young African elite, where Christianity most pointedly falters, there are, as in Nigeria, vigorous Islamic promotional campaigns of an inspirational and intellectual nature which have a most telling effect. In village areas Islam has a way of fitting itself snugly into the old social structures.

In teeming Lagos, a young Nigerian executive of a major oil company, a Ph.D. from New York University, told me of his leadership role in organizing a new Moslem association to appeal specifically to African intellectuals, especially to those just beginning their careers in government or industry. It was in Lagos, too, that Billy Graham was challenged to a public debate by a noted Moslem scholar, and, in keeping with his usual policy on such matters, refused. A typical comment is: "If Graham wanted to attack the Moslem faith, he had every right to do so; but he also should have had the courage to debate his views publicly."

Actually, forces deeper than a transient revolt against colonialism-tainted Christianity are working in Islam's favor. One such force is Moslem acceptance of polygamy under conditions which make sense to many Africans. Plural marriage dies a natural economic death in the city, where it is simply too expensive and unwieldy, but in the village areas it is viewed by Africans as an eminently sensible, practical, and natural arrangement.

Another powerful factor is the ease with which Moslem teachings may be learned. Christian doctrines, on the other hand, strike many Africans as being both incomprehensible and fanciful. Moreover, Christianity involves simple reflexes which are contrary to deeply ingrained African customs. In Africa, a visitor might show respect for his host's home by removing his shoes; but when he enters a Christian church, he is expected to bare his head.

The strongest factor of all, however, is probably the basic question of color. Islam groans under no burden of being first and foremost a white man's religion. If there is any color consciousness at all in Islamic life, it is directed at those of the palest skins.

In fairness to Christian efforts in Africa, it should be said that much of the current criticism is inspired by the xenophobic side of African Nationalism, which, for the present at least, strongly reacts against everything associated with the colonial era. It is not unusual, however, for Islam to be caught in this same cross-fire.

Typical of the many religious movements which reject *both* Christianity and Islam is one in Nigeria called Natural Religion of Africa. Mr. B. A. Oji, the self-styled General President of this enterprise, claims two thousand followers. He told me that his movement considers the Christian profession of "goodwill toward men" to be meaningless, because Christianity "has proved itself in practice to be a quarrelsome religion, each denomination attacking the other."

As he told me this, my mind jumped to an experience in a Ghanaian village where the head man informed me that he considered "all this Christian palaver to be for children." He backed up his opinion by revealing one of his gravest village problems. "About a third of my people are Methodists," he said. "About a third are Presbyterians. The rest are, of course, what I would call African in religion. Whenever we try to settle a village issue without reverting to the old clan and family structure, the Methodists and Presbyterians are at one another's throats. To get anything done we have to stop, tell the Methodists and Presbyterians to forget their religion, and go back to the old clan and family pattern of making decisions."

But to return to Mr. Oji. It is his claim that both Christianity and Islam failed to bring peace, love and unity to African life, and that the only religion suitable for the African soul is one "rooted in African culture and fostered by Africans."

Mr. Oji—and he is by no means alone in this—quite vehemently considers it un-African to be a Christian or a Moslem. And it should be emphasized that he is not a crank, or a fanatic, or a crackpot. He is widely respected in eastern Nigeria as a dedicated educator and as a tireless crusader against graft and governmental corruption, no small problems in emerging Africa.

The fact remains that Christianity is in deep trouble in Africa. As the Archbishop of York wrote after a recent African tour: "Time is short." It is shorter in some places than in others, but it would be foolhardy for the major Christian bodies not to recognize that Christian work in Africa needs sweeping renovation for a totally new era of African history.

In religion, as in politics, Africans seem determined to cut a coat to their own measure. The prevailing mood is one of resentment against whatever divides and sets African against African. Africa is undergoing a spiritual revolution as well as the more familiar "revolution of rising expectations," and the ways in which African peoples talk about religious matters are in marked contrast to the old framework in which missionary work was undertaken. There is excitement in Africa today in the spiritual as well as the political realm, and there is shattering dislocation of soul, especially among the young. Much that sounds now like denunciation and scathing criticism is actually a sort of thinking out loud about themselves, about their own aching hopes and painful fears. When they speak so belligerently of their proud heritage of the past, they really seem to mean that their future must somehow be built on the foundations of their own religious and cultural traditions. "To us Africans," one said to me, "history starts today, yet today grows out of yesterday—our yesterday, not yours."

II

The Great Gods of Africa

ON March 19, 1960, Philip Kgosana, a Transvaaler, was a shy, wispy twenty-year-old, who paid his rent by selling *Contact*, a liberal South African fortnightly newspaper. At *Contact*'s offices it was known that he attended Cape Town University, that he kept accurate accounts, and that he was pleasant enough when spoken to. Otherwise, Philip Kgosana was just another tall, thin, taciturn African.

On March 20, 1960, Philip Kgosana threw up his career at the University (a privilege of great price) and launched a campaign that shook Cape Town.

On an improvised platform in the African township of Langa, he stood before several thousand of his black countrymen and told them that at exactly 7 A.M. the next day they would begin a "Positive Decisive Action against the Pass Laws."

Philip Kgosana had never led anything in his life, but the people listening to him knew that they were listening to an inspired man. His eloquence was transforming:

"At this stage of our struggle we have a choice before us.

Are we still prepared to be half-human beings in our fatherland, or are we prepared to be citizens—men and women in a democratic nonracial South Africa? How long shall we be Bantu, Native, Non-European, Non-White, or black, stinking Kaffir in our fatherland? When shall we be called Sir, Mr., Mrs., Miss, Ladies and Gentlemen? How long shall we stay in the squalors of Windermere or the Sahara Desert of Nyanga West? How long shall we starve amidst plenty in our fatherland? How long shall we be rightless, voteless and voiceless eleven millions in our fatherland?

"On what meat doth this our oppressive White Man Boss feed that he has grown so great? Sons and daughters of Africa—there is a choice before us. We are either slaves or free men—that's all."

Kgosana was prepared to do more than stir the emotions with eloquence. He had a program and he spelled it out:

"I want to be properly understood here. Let the world take note that we are not fighting Dr. Verwoerd simply because he is Dr. Verwoerd; we are not fighting against the Nationalist Party or the United Party. We are not fighting against Europeans or Indians or Chinese. In short, we are fighting against nobody. Our energies and forces are directed against a setup, against a conception and a myth. This myth —others call it racial superiority, others call herrenvolkism, others white leadership with justice, or white supremacy. We are fighting against the Calvinistic doctrine that a certain Nation was specially chosen by God to lead, guide and protect other Nations.

"We are not a horde of stupid, barbaric things which will fight against a white man simply because he is white. No sensible person can do that. In order to destroy this myth of race superiority, the Pan-Africanist Congress has drawn up an unfolding program—which starts tomorrow and ends up in 1963 with the realization of the United States of Africa.

We start with the Pass Laws, then the next thing and the next."

After indicating in some detail how the campaign against the Pass Laws was to be carried out, Kgosana told his audience what they were *not* going to do:

"We are not going to burn or damage any part of the Pass Book in any manner. We are not going to fight or attempt to fight, insult or attempt to insult, provoke or attempt to provoke the police in their lawful duties. We are not going to throw stones at the police or do anything that is going to obstruct the police. Any person who does all these things shall be dealt with by the police of course and we, as an organization, shall further deal with him. Nobody is carrying money, knives or any dangerous weapon with himself tomorrow.

"People are not going to join this struggle with evil personal interests in it. Nobody is going to burn any building, office or school, or any property of the government. Nobody is going to cut wires or make attempts to cut railway lines. Nobody is going to burn any bus or threaten anybody.

"If anybody does all these things and the police begin to shoot, any person who will die or receive injuries shall be demanded on the head of the mischief-maker. *The Gods of Africa shall pass judgment on such a person* [italics mine].

"The same applies to the police. We do not want to be provoked in any manner. We do not want to be given impossible instructions such as—disperse in three minutes—or some such mumbled orders. If the police want us to disperse we shall disperse. Our leaders will always be on the spot to tell us what to do. We do not want to be tossed about. If they baton charge us we shall not run away but we will not fight back. We shall leave them to the judgment of the eyes of the world and *to the great Gods of Africa* [italics mine]."

On March 21, Kgosana's campaign did begin. It was conducted just as he said it would be conducted. His discipline over his followers was superb. He himself was imprisoned, but on March 25 he was released, and was carried back to Langa on the shoulders of his adherents. Five days later he led the now-famous peaceful march of the 30,000 into the heart of Cape Town, to ask that he be granted an audience with the authorities to discuss the Africans' grievances. Once again his masterful leadership held sway. There were no insults, no fighting, no stone-throwing, no provocation. No weapons were carried. The 30,000 marched past the golf course, through shopping areas, past white men's homes—and there was no violence! Shopkeepers came out to watch without barring their windows or doors; ponderous twin-deck buses were waved through the crowd; cars moved among them. They walked fast, Kgosana on ahead in sandals, dark shorts, an open-collar white shirt, and a sweater and jacket—his head high, his long arms swinging.

Through Athlone and Mowbray they went, up onto the De Waal Drive. The sun shone—there was no fear or bitterness: It was a friendly, almost joyful atmosphere.

At the foot of the De Waal Drive, Kgosana stopped them. He asked them to sit down in the shade and listen to him. He told them that he was going to walk on with five others to ask for an interview with the Minister of Justice. They must wait in peace. As he was leaving, people asked if he was not afraid of arrest. He voiced complete confidence in this attempt to achieve a just solution of legitimate grievances through consultation with the authorities.

In front of Caledon Square a large crowd had assembled from all over the city. Kgosana went up the steps of the Caledon Square Police Station and was promised his interview.

Still quietly, he led his men out of Cape Town, back to

Langa. At this "the great Gods of Africa" must have been pleased.

Philip Kgosana did not get his interview; instead, he was arrested. At this "the great Gods of Africa" must have been dismayed.

I tell this story for two reasons: In the first place, it is a tale out of Africa which is all too little known—in our part of the world at least—in its stark and vibrant detail. Its protagonist, Kgosana, will be heard from again. More than a year after his betrayal and imprisonment by South African authorities, he escaped, made his way through the African underground, literally by walking up the continent, and finally arrived safely in Tanganyika. From there he was flown to London to join other exiles from "the fatherland."

A more compelling reason, for the purposes of this book, is to clothe with flesh and blood the inherited outlook of such Africans—the makers of their continent's future—as Philip Kgosana. "The great Gods of Africa," to whose judgment he assigned the behavior both of his followers and the South African police, are obviously real to those who invoke them, and play some deep, fundamental role in the emergence of many African leadership personalities. Philip Kgosana could not possibly have made his way to Cape Town University without a great deal of exposure to Christian education and affiliation. Yet, when he stood there on the platform in Langa, with the mantle of charismatic leadership suddenly and mysteriously upon his shoulders (and displaying, incidentally, a sophisticated acquaintance with Calvinist doctrine), he invoked not the God of Abraham, Isaac, and Joseph—not God the Father, Son, and Holy Ghost—but *the great Gods of Africa.* A leader in Africa, like leaders in all cultures, must understand and be understood by his people, working within a framework of popular traditions and convictions. This, puzzling though his sudden emergence may be to those who do not share his heritage, is obviously a role for which Kgosana is spiritually prepared.

To the outsider, Africa does not seem to have a self-evident, unifying spiritual heritage, as have other assertive parts of the world—the Arab states, for example, or India, or Burma. Yet, the modern African leader—detribalized and uprooted though he seems to be by European domination—exhibits over and over again this ability to touch the taproots of an African spirit.

One of South Africa's oldest jokes is about a "non-European," as Africans are commonly described by the white authorities. "Where do you come from?" a white policeman asks this non-European. "I come from non-Europe," he replies.

This feeling of belonging to "non-Europe" pervades the whole of Africa, and its extension is a sense of belonging body and soul to a *positive* entity: *Africa.* If "the great Gods of Africa" preside over this entity, then who are they, and what do they represent?

Someone has said that the only generalization one may safely make about Africa is that it is a continent. I am convinced that it is also reasonably safe to make some generalizations about traditional African spiritual beliefs. It can be said, for example, that the inherited ancient religions of Africa are best described as polytheistic: the worship of, or concern with, many gods and spirits. There is, of course, nothing especially remarkable about this. Similar patterns held sway in ancient Greece, Egypt, India, and elsewhere. What is striking about Africa is that on a continent so vast, so chopped up tribally, so lacking in a coherent history, there yet emerges a nearly universal pattern of revered spirits and spiritual forces. The names of these spirits and spiritual forces are as varied as Africa's multitudinous tribal languages, but the system, virtually everywhere, can be described in a three-fold manner: a supreme God; lesser gods and spirits; and spirits of the dead.

Among the Yoruba of western Nigeria, the creator God is variously called Father and Lord, Almighty, Owner of Breath or Spirit, Chief of Glory. He is believed to be the creator of all things, the judge of men now and after death, and the sustainer of the moral law. In the Yoruba tongue the words *adake-dajo* give to this supreme God's judicial function a fascinating "silent but active" character. The most revered of his proper names is *Olorun,* which means "owner of heaven."

A traditional Yoruba believer holds that his soul must render to God an account of its mortal deeds; that the righteous go to the "good heaven" and the wicked to the "heaven of potsherds," that is, a rubbish heap.

The lesser divinities depend upon Olorun. He is their source and their awesome superior. Yet one can trek the length and breadth of Yoruba land and find no temple where Olorun is worshipped. Other gods have their temples and priests, but not the supreme God; other gods have their festival occasions, but not Olorun.

Intrigued and puzzled by this, a great student of West African religion, Geoffrey Parrinder, ferreted about for an explanation. Is Olorum such a vague and remote God that he could disappear from Yoruba theology and not be missed? The priest of one important temple, when quizzed on this point, answered that he did not worship Olorun, but that he believed God created his own temple deity (*Oduduwa*). He said that "before Europeans came to this country, the Yoruba people knew of God, but built Him no temples, but that nowadays anybody who has money can build a house for Him—that is to say, a church or mosque."

A priest of *Orishala* took another tack when questioned.

He told Parrinder that all his prayers "ended with the name of God, usually the name used is Almighty or Chief of All (*Oludumare*). At the end of prayers to other gods it is said 'God will do it' (*Olorun a she e*), meaning that whatever remains undone will be finished by God."

Parrinder also discovered that people frequently broke kola nuts and poured water libations outside their houses for Olorun in times of emergency or grave need. Their explanation was that when other gods have failed, it is necessary and prudent to appeal to the greatest of all. It was not unusual, during illnesses, for family members to put out a portion of cold meal for God and give the rest, after suitable prayers, to the sick person. Elders told Parrinder that such prayers were said in the open air, because "no one knows where the face of God is to be found." Some said this was a reason why Olorun had no man-made temples. Since God is everywhere, it is foolish to try to confine Him to a temple.

Parrinder's discoveries are remarkably similar to those made by observers of other African tribal groups. Invariably there is a supreme God. Many speak his name as they prepare for sleep, "May God wake us up well"; and when they arise they say, "God grant us food." He is believed in. His existence and presence are real and majestic. Why then do not Africans worship Him alone? The real answer seems to be that in the African view it would be foolish to neglect the lesser powers, who are much closer, much more watchful, and therefore potentially both more troublesome than the supreme God and more serviceable in a crisis. That all men *can* call upon God, Africans readily agree; but why waste what might well be a limited store of final appeals?

Chinua Achebe is an Ibo of eastern Nigeria. In his first novel, *Things Fall Apart*, he tells of conditions in a village at the turn of the century after the first Christian missionaries came. Whenever Mr. Brown, the area mission supervisor, visited the village, he spent many hours with the head man, Akunna, in his *obi,* discussing religion through an interpreter. Neither of them got very far in changing the other's beliefs, but they did learn more about their different beliefs:

"You say that there is one supreme God who made heaven and earth," said Akunna on one of Mr. Brown's visits. "We also believe in Him and call Him Chukwu. He made all the world and the other gods."

"There are no other gods," said Mr. Brown. "Chukwu is the only God and all the others are false. You carve a piece of wood —like that one" (he pointed at the rafters from which Akunna's carved *Ikenga* hung), "and you call it a god. But it is still a piece of wood."

"Yes," said Akunna. "It is indeed a piece of wood. The tree from which it came was made by Chukwu, as indeed all minor gods were. But He made them for His messengers so that we could approach Him through them. It is like yourself. You are the head of your church."

"No," protested Mr. Brown. "The head of my church is God Himself."

"I know," said Akunna, "but there must be a head in this world among men. Somebody like yourself must be the head here."

"The head of my church in that sense is in England."

"That is exactly what I am saying. The head of your church is in your country. He has sent you here as his messenger. And you have also appointed your own messengers and servants. Or let me take another example, the District Commissioner. He is sent by your king."

"They have a queen," said the interpreter on his own account.

"Your queen sends her messenger, the District Commissioner. He finds that he cannot do the work alone and so he appoints *kotma* to help him. It is the same with God, or Chukwu. He appoints the smaller gods to help Him because His work is too great for one person."

"You should not think of him as a person," said Mr. Brown. "It is because you do so that you imagine He must need helpers. And the worst thing about it is that you give all the worship to the false gods you have created."

"That is not so. We make sacrifices to the little gods, but when they fail and there is no one else to turn to, we go to Chukwu. It is right to do so. We approach a great man through his servants. But when his servants fail to help us, then we go to the last source of hope. We appear to pay greater attention to the little gods but that is not so. We worry them more because we are afraid to worry their Master. Our fathers knew that Chukwu was the Overlord and that is why many of them gave their children the name Chukwu—'Chukwu is Supreme.' "

"You said one interesting thing," said Mr. Brown. "You are afraid of Chukwu. In my religion Chukwu is a loving Father and need not be feared by those who do His will."

"But we must fear Him when we are not doing His will," said Akunna. "And who is to tell His will? It is too great to be known."

On Akunna's final point, about the necessity of fearing Chukwu, I recall the words of a brilliant Ghanaian, one of the most promising and energetic of Ghana's native Methodist leaders. We were discussing ways in which mission teaching had failed to take account of African outlooks. What he said went something like this: "When I was growing up, my elders used to tell me that Christianity had brought about a lowering of moral standards in Africa because the Christian God was too good! This may sound like a silly charge, but the more I think of it, the more I become convinced the fault lies in an oversentimentalized idea of the love of God. There have been two extremes in the presentation of God. The good old Methodist preachers used to practically will down hell-fire. Then the pendulum swung to the other extreme; the love of God was now emphasized at the expense of His wrath. To most people in Africa the Supreme Being is good, but He does not brook evil and wickedness."

A certain light is here thrown upon Philip Kgosana's ominous prophecy that "the great Gods of Africa" would pass judgment on all who violated the peaceful methods of action against the Pass Laws.

In summary, there can be no doubt that belief in a high or supreme God is widely spread in Africa. It used to be said that the presence of such ideas must be due to the influence of Christian missionaries and Moslem preachers, but it is well known now that the notion of a Supreme Being did not come from the outside. It is a part of ancient African life; indeed, missionaries found that the Judeo-Christian God was something reasonably familiar to Africans. The more one talks with ordinary Africans, old and young, the deeper the impression grows of an age-old relationship existing between men and an almighty, creator God, who is the maker of gods and men.

In a welter of mangrove-poles and wattle houses live the Kalabari, an Ijo-speaking, fishing people of the eastern Niger Delta.

Their highest enthusiasms are devoted to religious activities, and their fondest admiration is reserved for those who excel in the dancing, drumming, and other skills associated with the spiritual life. In this respect, as in many others, Kalabari are typical of Africa's massive rural population. Their view of the gods' place in the world is literally the key to their lives.

Kalabari theology splits the world into two orders of being: that of *oju* (the physical or material), and that of *teme* (the spiritual or nonmaterial). Whatever has *oju* can be seen by anyone who is in a position to do so, because *oju*, whether as man, fish, snake, tree, grass, or stone, always occupies definite locations in space.

Teme, on the other hand, can be seen by ordinary people

only when they are very young, before the corruptions of the material world have destroyed clairvoyance.

This lost faculty can be recaptured, but only by those willing to submit to a drastic herbal therapy known as "clearing the eyes and ears." Thus are recruited the diviners, who are capable of engaging *teme* in conversation and learning their will.

Though *teme* are sometimes spoken of as coming to a certain place and remaining there, they are also described as being everywhere and anywhere "like the breeze." It is possible for *teme* to exist without any bodily counterparts in the *oju* world: the village hero-gods and the dead, for example. These are "the people we do not see." But everything having *oju* also has a counterpart in *teme*. When a person or animal loses *teme*, it dies. This process applies to all objects of the ordinary world, animate or inanimate, even to a particular set of gods known as the Water People. *Teme* controls *oju* as a helmsman controls a fishing boat.

In theory all *teme* may be worshipped, appeased, or pacified through prayer or offerings. The Kalabari say that "if one cuts a stick and pours wine before it, the stick becomes a god." The stick does, after all, have a *teme*. In everyday practice, however, only a limited selection of *teme* are considered to be powerful enough to justify much effort. As might be expected, not all Kalabari agree on which *teme* to heed and which to neglect. The more tender-minded feel obliged to make offerings to the *teme* of various parts of their houses, while those made of sterner stuff consider household *teme* of too little significance to be worth the bother.

An outlook quite foreign to the Western mind but nearly universal in traditional African religions is typified by the Kalabari saying, "It is men who make the gods great." The power of a god is strengthened by human attentions. The more fervent the worship, the more potent the god's ability to aid the worshipper. The Yoruba word for prayer is *she orisha,* to "make" the god. When Kalabari pray to a god, they share in the god's life force; it helps them to achieve a higher life. But, by the same token, the force of the god is renewed by the prayers, and thus the community helps to rejuvenate the god's powers.

Sometimes a god begins to behave maliciously and has to be put in his place. He has to be "diminished." As an example, one old Kalabari fisherman tells of the village of Owome, where the people worshipped a Water Man known as *Akpana.* It was known that Akpana frequently assumed the *oju* of a shark, and after several Owome fishermen had been eaten by sharks, the community appealed to its diviners for help. After deliberate study they reported back that Akpana was the culprit. The council of chiefs took immediate steps to put an end to the Water Man's capricious and unwarranted intrusions: They decreed the capture of a shark, whose blood was poured into the village well. In solemn ceremony each man drank a draught of the "spiked" well water. The confidently believed result of this symbolic act of community rejection was the curtailment of Akpana's power to do *either* good or evil.

When questioned as to how the rituals of men can affect the strength of a god, Kalabari explain that it is, after all, the same with mortals, whose *teme* become strong and vital, or weak and lazy, in proportion to the honor they are accorded by their fellows. Western inability to understand such matters has long been a source of sad head-shaking in Africa: "White men are really amazingly naïve. They have learned to invent all kinds of marvels, yet they have no intelligence. They understand nothing about the gods!"

The aphorism "man proposes, but God disposes" would make little sense to a Kalabari priest. The gods exist to share their powers with men. If the prayers and offerings of worshippers do not bring the desired benefits, there can be only two explanations: Either the diviner has directed suppliants to the wrong god, or the ritual itself has been incorrectly performed.

Kalabari differ about the relative prowess of some *teme*, but there are two families of gods whose power and influence command the respect of all.

In the first group are what might be called the Arbiters of Form and Process. In the beginning the supreme God of creation found two forces with which to work: One was the female principle *Tamuno;* the other the male principle *So*. From *Tamuno* came the earth, and to *So* was given the direction of the earth. Everything in the world has its particular portion of *Tamuno* and *So*. The life course of each village, each compound, each individual, is created and controlled by its respective *Tamuno* and *So*.

An individual's destiny, say the Kalabari, is "what he spoke before he came." And again the Westerner is confused. But the sophistication of the saying emerges as it is explained. Before his birth a person's *teme* goes to tell his *Tamuno* what course of life he chooses. *Tamuno* hears these words and cherishes them. The words, personified, become the *So* or destiny of the person whose *teme* came before her to speak. She then sends the *teme* to merge with a body which she has created in a mother's womb. How supremely logical it is, then, that a person is "what he spoke before he came."

While there are as many *Tamuno* and as many *So* as there are people or objects in the world, yet the various *Tamuno* are one great *Tamuno,* and the various *So* are one great *So*. The unity and diversity or life are thus self-contained, and everything in the world can be explained by *Tamuno* and *So,* acting in their various roles.

We will see in a moment that the style of thought which

sustains ideas of *Tamuno* and *So* is quite different from that which concerns itself with the second family of gods. *Tamuno* and *So* are principles of a rarified and abstract nature: creation and control of process. Apart from these functions they have no vivid personalities, no bluster, no laughter, neither love nor wrath. As one highly educated Kalabari expressed it: "*Tamuno* and *So* are gods many an atomic physicist could respect."

The second group of gods is another matter, for here we come upon the Village Heroes, the Water People, and the Ancestors. With each of these we enter into the human, everyday experiences of life, and find explanations for everything that happens in the Kalabari world.

First, the Village Heroes, who exist today in *teme* only. The time was, however, when they lived among the founders of Kalabari villages in full-blown *oju* form, and a delightful mythology preserves in vast detail their deeds and personalities during their bodily existence.

The Village Heroes, it is told, came to help found Kalabari villages from far distant places. Their purpose in coming was to teach Kalabari pioneers all kinds of necessary skills. To the villagers of Owome, for example, the skills of trade were brought and taught by *Owamekaso*. Dancing and drumming for the masquerade were the special talents of *Ekine ba*. Prowess in various types of war and head-hunting was the specialty of *Okpolodo* and *Siriopudo*. The indispensable arts of curing and cleansing were imported by *Amakarasa* and *Kugbosa*.

What more could a pioneer community ask! Yet it is said that the Village Heroes of Owome soon became weary of their adopted but backsliding people. The villagers, it seems, persisted in breaking tabus laid down by the Heroes as essential to the skills in which they specialized. Repeated warnings were given, but ignored. Then, one by one, the Heroes simply disappeared—vanished.

They did not fly off into the sky, however, without leaving behind detailed instructions about the prayers and offerings to be made to them, in return for which they would continue to look after Owome's welfare. They would do this in the future, however, as *teme*. The Heroes forsook *oju* forever. The responsibility for guarding and cherishing the cults was entrusted to the descendants of certain village men whom the Heroes had befriended during their bodily existence. But the cults were to be carried on for the benefit of the community as a whole.

Secondly, there are the Water People who play a role both different and complementary to that of the Village Heroes. Their concern is not with the invention and maintenance of human skills, but with the control of Nature, whose fluctuations outstrip and defy all human skills. Their special task is to master the water level, the waves in the creek, and the movements and depths of the fish shoals. Every Water Man patrols his own tract of creek or shore-line. His domain has clearly marked geographical boundaries, and woe to the fishermen who do not know in what Water Man's realm they cast their nets.

The Water People no less than the Village Heroes are honored with an elaborate mythology recounting their rich and varied life in the towns below the creek beds, and explaining how the Kalabari first became acquainted with them. But there is none of the intimacy associated with the Village Heroes. The Water People never lived in *oju* form among the villagers. Their contacts with men involve no particular communal loyalties, thus Akpana, as we have seen, could be thought of by the chiefs of Owome as being responsible for malicious mischief against the village. In fact, the Water People, because their concern is chiefly with their own domains, can be approached by anyone or any village. And they are likely to sell their favors to the highest bidder. It is the Water People, never the Village Heroes or the Ancestors, who are thought useful for advancing individual careers.

Finally, the Ancestors—the Dead—are the *teme* of human beings which slipped from their bodies at death and continue their existence in the nonmaterial world. Their personalities and values are believed to be the same as when alive, and their relations to one another are similar to those of living Kalabari. Like the Village Heroes and the Water People, they are woven about with a vivid mythology, but they occupy themselves neither with villages nor with individuals. Their concern is with the collective welfare of the extended families to which they gave birth. Whatever good or ill may befall a family is generally explained by the activities and attitudes of the Dead.

Yet the Dead are not alive! That is, they are not alive in the sense that we of the West think of aliveness. The Dead exist; therefore they are not "dead." They exist, and their existence communicates itself to their living descendants with vibrant force. Jahnheinz Jahn quotes the Senegambian poet, Birago Diop, in what is a superb illustration of the African concept of the continued existence of the Dead:

> Hear more often things than beings,
> the voice of the fire listening,
> hear the voice of the water.
> Hear in the wind
> the bushes sobbing,
> it is the sigh of our forbears.
>
> Those who are dead are never gone:
> they are there in the thickening shadow.
> The dead are not under the earth:

they are in the tree that rustles,
they are in the wood that groans,
they are in the water that runs,
they are in the water that sleeps,
they are in the hut, they are in the crowd,
the dead are not dead.

Those who are dead are never gone,
they are in the breast of the woman,
they are in the child who is wailing
and in the firebrand that flames.
The dead are not under the earth:
they are in the fire that is dying,
they are in the grasses that weep,
they are in the whimpering rocks,
they are in the forest, they are in the house,
the dead are not dead.

We have used the Kalabari (and I trust they will not mind that we have so used them) to illustrate the "wholeness" with which a typical African people has worked out its relationship to being. The Village Heroes and the Water People fit together into a trim, complementary system of influence over human skills and Nature's forces, while families are watched over and guided by the ever-present Dead. Together, these three groups of gods provide explanation and control of every situation in the material world. The triumvirate, in its own way, is as self-contained as the system made up of the Arbiters of Form and Process. In fact, the Village Heroes, the Water People, and the Dead form a complete alternative to *Tamuno* and *So!* What is more, there lies behind them a totally contrasting style of thought. The two systems are as unlike in religious psychology as Martin Luther and Benedict Spinoza. Against the austere, abstract background of *Tamuno* and *So*, the folk and ancestor gods loom up in full-blooded personalities.

How, we ask, in a people presumed by so many of us to be "barely above savagery," can we explain such elaborate and paradoxical thought? The basic answer, of course, is that Africans are neither more nor less than people who differ from us in nothing that is essential to humanity. Their religious responses to life are those of the human spirit striving to comprehend and to control. The Kalabari, like peoples everywhere on the globe, came to believe a long time ago that gods exist, and that they are responsive to men who approach them correctly. Such guarantees are an ageless source of man's peace of mind in an unpredictable and threatening universe. The Kalabari, as must all men, also faced the fact of inevitable failure in many of their approaches to the gods. This is an exceedingly nasty threat, and it shrieks for some solution, no matter how fanciful. The Kalabari followed familiar human paths when they laid the blame for their failures on errors committed against the iron rules of correct ritual. The Old Testament book of Leviticus relates the savage retribution meted out by Jehovah when Nadab and Abihu, sons of the high priest Aaron, made the sad mistake of offering *strange fire* in one of their rituals. They were immediately consumed by flames.

But there is always hope in a corrected performance. Students of the American Indian will recall that the Navaho specialized in fantastically complicated rituals, in which the possibility of error was virtually limitless. The Kalabari, and Africans generally, are much more conservative. Their ritual procedures offer some—but not too much—scope for the "out" of human error. Instead, they acknowledge that more than one system of gods may be involved in any given situation. This makes it possible for Kalabari to explain failure of worship by the notion that prayers or offerings have apparently been made to the wrong *teme*.

With the diviner rests the glory and risk of identifying the *right teme,* and everyone knows that diviners can on occasion be mistaken, or even fraudulent. So failure is not final. There is always hope that another "doctor" will "see more clearly" what is required, and put the suppliants in touch with the god who is really concerned.

To have *two* ways of explaining a world of pain and joy is obviously better than one, but we may still be puzzled over why these two ways should differ so radically in tone and style. Yet, is it odd? The same Europe produced Luther and Spinoza. For that matter, the same America embraces Oral Roberts and Paul Tillich. The gods of any community are bound to reflect the human genius for diversity. So wide-ranging are any people's desires and interests that their gods are more likely than not to be molded in contradictory patterns.

The two systems of Kalabari gods may seem incompatible with one another, but they are not incompatible with diverse Kalabari desires and interests. Both arise from a longing to explain situations as a prelude to controlling them. As elsewhere, however, there are Kalabari who yearn for explanations of life quite apart from their desire to control it. All Westerners who have lived for any length of time in African villages are struck by the discovery that every village has its cool, collected men of abstractions. Of supreme interest to such people everywhere in the world is tidiness and comprehensiveness of explanation—with a few clear but sweeping principles to be able to embrace everything that happens in the world. The Arbiters of Form and Process, *Tamuno* and *So*—the austere, impersonal gods of Kalabari religion—ideally answer the needs of such people.

The writings of the great Roman Catholic philosophers carry the reader into rarefied realms of proof that God is the unchanging, unchangeable, primary, necessary, perfect and intelligent cause of all that happens in the world of experienced fact and event. But the observer of the everyday practices of ordinary Catholic communicants sees a welter of ritual acts which are far more concerned with Mary and the Saints than with God.

The desire to participate actively in the society of supernatural beings produces a thirst quite different from that of the philosophically minded. This thirst is stronger in some cultures than in others, and stronger among some members of a particular culture than among other members. There are African tribes—the Nupe for example—where the gods are habitually treated as faceless forces swaying man and nature, and hardly ever as *personalities.* Among the Kalabari the reverse is true. It is the gods as tangible persons, full of intense feelings and emotions, who attract the fancy and loyalty of most Kalabari.

Still, this drive to develop the gods as full-blooded persons must conflict with the desire of other Kalabari for neatness and breadth of interpretation. So there is no unifying possibility other than the one Kalabari wisely adopt: the coexistence of two systems of gods fashioned in completely contrasting styles. In this way Kalabari are able to give their contradictory spiritual impulses free rein.

Tamuno and *So,* gods without faces, are granted a quiet, passionless devotion. Offerings are made and invocations spoken. The matter is then allowed to rest until the results are in. But with the Village Heroes, the Water People and the Dead, worship takes on an exuberant, warm-blooded tone. The sentiments drawn upon are the richest of which the Kalabari are capable. Ritual days are times of ardent expectancy, and the melodies of women chanters resound through the villages, praising the gods for their prowess and achievements.

The Ghanaian poet, Francis Ernest Kobina Parkes, has attempted to catch the spirit of such African village expectancy in a poem especially tuned to the Western ear:

Give me some drums;
Let them be three
Or maybe four
And make them black–
Dirty and black:
Of wood,
And dried sheepskin,
But if you will
Just make them peal,
Peal.
Peal loud,
Mutter.
Loud,
Louder yet;
Then soft,
Softer still
Let the drums peal.
Let the calabash
Entwined with beads
With blue Aggrey beads
Resound, wildly
Discordant,
Calmly
Melodious.
Let the calabash resound
In tune with the drums.
Mingle with these sounds
The clang
Of wood on tin:
Kententsekenen
Ken-tse ken ken ken:
Do give me voices
Ordinary
Ghost voices

Voices of women
And the bass
Of men
(And screaming babes?)

Let there be dancers,
Broad-shouldered Negroes
Stamping the ground
With naked feet
And half-covered
Women
Swaying, to and fro
In perfect
Rhythm
To '*Tom shikishiki*'
And 'ken,'
And voices of ghosts
Singing,
Singing!
Let there be
A setting sun above,
Green palms
Around,
A slaughtered fowl
And plenty of
Yams.

And dear Lord,
If the place be
Not too full,
Please admit
Admit spectators.
They may be
White or
Black.

Admit spectators
That they may

See:
The bleeding fowl,
And yams,
And palms
And dancing ghosts.

Odomankoma,
Do admit spectators
That they may
Hear:
Our native songs,
The clang of wood on tin
The tune of beads
And the pealing drums.

Twerampon, please, please
Admit
Spectators!
That they may
Bask
In the balmy rays
Of the
Evening Sun
In our lovely
African heaven!

Were we to come as spectators to a Kalabari village at ritual time, we would hear the invocations, view the offerings, and then witness the most exciting of Kalabari religious practices, the dramatization of the gods' presence! Human actors dance out sequences of behavior which in one way or another exemplify the deeds and special characteristics of the gods—the most momentous means, as Kalabari understand it, of actually bringing the gods into the village. During such a dramatization, the villagers behave as if the gods *are indeed* present as exalted guests who merit the very best in entertainment and hospitality. The Kalabari speak of this as "playing with the gods."

It is easy to understand why *Tamuno* and *So* are not visualized as sprightly village guests. Their abstruse qualities would be extremely difficult to dramatize in any of the ways familiar to Kalabari. The Village Heroes, the Water People and the Dead, on the other hand, are marvelous subjects for skilled portrayal.

Kalabari actors "bring the gods into the village" in three different ways. The first technique is simple *impersonation,* in which an actor merely mimics the character and attributes of a god. The technique of *masquerading* is next. Once again the character and attributes of a god are acted out, but now the actor is garbed in clothing and a mask which also symbolize the god. The most cherished of the three techniques is *possession,* in which the god is believed to "come into a man's head" during the performance and temporarily to replace the *teme* in control of the dancer's body.

A normal reaction for an outsider is to wonder how Kalabari can believe that *impersonation* and *masquerading* can be as effective as *possession* for bringing the gods into close contact with their people. *Possession* has a convincing eeriness about it which is absent from the other techniques. Still, the Kalabari closely relate all three in their thinking.

The key to this mystery is found in the Kalabari saying, "It is with their names that the gods stay and come." Here the Kalabari are intensely typical of one of the near-universals of African thought. It is a quality about which Janheinz Jahn has written so effectively in his book *Muntu*—a quality described by the Bantu term *Nommo:* the magic power of the word. According to this African view, it is man alone in the material world who possesses intellect, active intelligence. This intelligence is of two kinds: cleverness and wisdom. A child is intelligent in the first sense. He is capable of learning. But wisdom comes only with a true understanding of the nature and relationships of the world. And this, as Jahn points out, includes "the knowledge of the manner in which . . . human intelligence makes use of . . . 'things' and activates the forces asleep in them."

Jahn goes on to say that as early as 1603 there was a published report which anticipated a still-prevalent misunderstanding by Westerners of African psychology. The report recounts how Dutch traders told Gold Coast Africans that Holland owed all its great material possessions to God. The Africans marveled at this and wondered why God had not similarly bestowed on them the blessings of "Linen cloth, ironware, basins or copperware and such like goods even as ye receive from your God?"

The Dutch, with pious practicality, were quick to point out that God was indeed bountiful to the Africans, bestowing upon them "their gold . . . the wine of the palm trees and fruit and grain of all sorts, fowl, oxen and goats. Item: bananas, iniamas and such like, such as were needful for the preserving of their life."

The Africans would have none of it. In fact, they protested briskly against the notion that God had been responsible for any of these things: ". . . they said that God did give unto them no gold but the earth did give it unto them when they did sow it and afterward at the right time did reap and gather it. And for the fruits, these the trees did give unto them which they themselves had planted. Item, the young goats or lambs did come from the old ones. The sea did give unto them fishes and they needs must catch them therein. So they would not allow that these and such like things did come from God but were brought forth from the earth and from the water and were gained by their labour."

Actually, this outlook is not unknown in practical circles in our part of the world, and it is typified by the joke about the new Maine parson who went calling. At the farm of one parishioner the clergyman made repeated comments about how the farmer "and the Lord" had done wonders with the fences, fields, barns, and livestock. The farmer took it as long as he could, then exploded: "Parson, you should have seen this place when the Lord was runnin' it by himself!"

While a Western theologian might consider the farmer to be guilty of vain pride, if not of blasphemy, an African would probably feel that he was showing signs of genuine wisdom. It is not God but man who plows, plants, and cultivates. It is not God but man who mends fences, builds barns, and feeds livestock. Yet it is more than manual labor which the earth requires if it is to yield its fruits. As Jahn expresses the African concept: "Man must do more than sow and reap, for the seed corn has of itself no activity of its own, it does nothing without the influence of man, it would not grow but would remain lying in the ground without his help, without the influence of human *ubwenge* (active reason). How does man accomplish this? Through *Nommo,* the life force, which produces all life, which influences 'things' in the shape of the *word.*"

The life force is everywhere and in everything. The uniqueness of man is that by his power over the *word* he calls forth and guides the life force. For man, this is the meaning of life: to receive the word, to invoke it, and to share it with other beings, human or divine, living or dead, *oju* or *teme.*

When the Kalabari say "It is with their names that the gods stay and come," the meaning of "name" covers any chant, invocation, mask, fetish, or dance sequence which symbolizes the god, as well as the god's literal name itself. All of these are *Nommo,* the life force, and by the very presence of the *word* ("with their names"), the presence of the desired god is achieved. The god's literal name may be sung three times; it may throb out three times from the drums:

the sculptor may fashion a new image; the actor may put on the carved headdress and dance the god's behavior—any and all of these bringing the god near by the power of the *word.*

Thus the magic power of the word—a crucial key to African psychology—clears the mystery of how the Kalabari can view *impersonation* and *masquerading* as the equals of actual *possession* for bringing the gods into the village. When the villagers "play" with a mimic, they are associating with a god no less than when they are confronted by an appointed medium who is deep in the ecstacies of *possession.* Moreover, in a system of thought that sees all manner of change being spurred by the power of the *word,* it is but a short dance step from the presence of a god called forth by *impersonation* and *masquerading* to actual *possession* by that same god.

Men and their activities, nature and its vital motions, rest on the prolific energy of the *word,* which is the life force itself. Those capable of applying active intelligence to the use of the *word* include living men, the dead and the gods, all bound together in an active interdependence of powers which beget and sustain the movements of life. In turn, this grand design stems from the creator and ultimate source of all life, the generator of *all* vital force, God.

By looking into the theology of a typical African tribal group, the Kalabari, we have striven for some insight into Philip Kgosana's summons of "the great Gods of Africa"—words, incidentally, which mark him, in the current African context, as a Pan-Africanist, an African nationalist dedicated to the spiritual rebirth of an African personality which is not "black European," but viable and genuinely African.

It is plain that Africans, like Kgosana, who make it into secondary schools and beyond, have come in contact with a very different world view than that which embraces Kalabari and other tribal religions. In fact, that traditional picture of the world is everywhere crumbling, slowly but inexorably, before the assaults of the new age. Yet it is just as plain that "the great Gods of Africa" invoke a mystique. The words have literal meanings for masses of Africans, and psychological meanings for the Kgosanas—the educated men, the leadership cadres. It is in the words themselves—despite their different meanings to those who are educated and those who are not—that leaders and followers meet, and together draw upon a spiritual heritage that is theirs, Africa's. The words "great Gods of Africa" mean that there *is* an African spiritual tradition, and that this tradition stands in judgment on those who now open their eyes to Africa's new destiny. The words do *not* mean an attempt to revive the past as it was. For Kgosana and his like they do not mean a return to literal polytheism. What these words say to us is that the African will have no more of the old notion that he is a man without a spiritual past. He has a spiritual past—rich, imaginative, vigorous, and vital. As the heir and successor to that past, he has the strength for his new beginnings.

Intelligent African leaders wish to integrate into the future what seems valuable from the past. They wish, in other words, to revitalize the African tradition rationally, and to assimilate into it whatever Western or other elements are demanded by modern times. This is an exceedingly tricky and difficult task, and it is helped neither by the masses of Africans who are caught up in the toils of witchcraft and magic, nor by those masses of non-Africans who love the kicks and shudders they get from reading of "the ancestral rituals of sorcery."

III

Ju Ju

An issue of *Life* magazine (April 21, 1961) carried a lusty article about African religion, in which there was much savoring of African "superstitions" and "sorcery." The same issue also contained a laudatory piece about a white South African golfer. With straight face and obvious respect, the article quoted the golfer's explanation of how he approached the Master's Golf Tournament (which he won): "The Lord wants me to win." Readers were informed, again with no sign of a quizzical demur, that the golfer in question was "certain that he had heard a message from above." It seems not to have occurred to the editors of *Life* that one man's "superstition" is another man's "reverence." Thus, by barriers higher and thicker than we know, are we kept from entering truly into one another's lives.

Nothing out of Africa so scandalizes and hypnotizes Westerners as the mysterious world of Ju Ju, a world that harbors magic, witchcraft, sorcery, and medicine. It would perhaps be well to indicate the sense in which I use the term Ju Ju. It is a phrase which, in spite of its disguise, is nothing more than the French word *joujou*, a "toy" or "doll," and it came into use because of the prevalence of images and charms in native African religions. In its broadest sense, Ju Ju includes all the mysterious, incomprehensible forces of Nature, but in its narrower sense it describes the magico-religious practices in the "bread and butter" realms of what we loosely call "primitive" life: curses, spells, omens, good and bad magic, and, above all, witchcraft.

Ju Ju, I confess, is not a satisfactory term for what is without doubt a most urgent, comprehensive and controversial aspect of African religion. It is resented by many Africans who, for fear of furthering the image of backward savages, would be happy to drop the term altogether. An alternative is fetish, but it is really no better. When Portuguese navigators and traders first visited West Africa, they found every native wearing some talisman—a "magic" horn, a small shell, a ring—that had been charged with spirit-power (conjured up by the *word*) and trusted to aid and protect in all kinds of emergencies. The Portuguese themselves were ardent wearers of medallions, crucifixes, and other sacred symbols which had been properly blessed by their priests and were credited with similar virtues. Quite rightly, they concluded that thc African trinkets were cousins of their own, and they called them by the same name—"feitico," which Anglicized becomes fetish.

Well, fetish, Ju Ju, or something else, what matters is that we take a look at a looming reality of African life, and that we do so not to be titillated but to be informed.

For the overwhelming majority of Africans there is no clear separation between magic and religion. The intermingling of the two continues even among some intellectuals. An American friend, who is married to a Ghanaian and has given several years of service to the Ghana government, told me of an interview he had with an educated Ghanaian youth who was anxious to continue his schooling in America. The young man, as an added credential, emphasized vigorously that he was a conscientious and devoted Christian. My friend noticed a copper Ju Ju ring on the boy's finger. Pointing to it he asked what kind of line the young man was giving him about being such a convinced Christian. "Oh," he said, "I believe with all my heart that God will punish anyone who tries to do me harm, but this ring keeps him from doing it in the first place!"

For us to laugh at this and thus to imply that magic does not exist, that evil intent could not bring disease or even death to a man unless he had a more powerful magic to forestall it, is simply to leave an African, even a Christian African, shrugging his shoulders at our blindness.

That massive spiritual authority, *Nommo,* rules. All the practices of magic fall back upon it. Unless conjured by the *word,* no Ju Ju ring, no amulet of twisted root, no "medicine" can be effective. Without the *word,* they have no activity at all. Without the *word,* no poison, no evil spell, no curse can harm an intended victim. They too are helpless until the *word* liberates their wicked force.

Everything that happens in the world, every evil and every good, is caught up in the interplay of *word* and *counterword.* Life is a unity saturated through and through with the presence of forces loosed by the *word,* and most Africans do nothing apart from their understanding of this. In childhood, maturity, or old age, whether cutting palm nuts, guiding the destinies of a government ministry, building a new thatched hut, buying a limousine, needing rain, or orating before a nationalist rally—everything an African does is related in his heritage to the spirit world of vital force, to *Nommo,* to the ever-present *word.*

So it is quite true that when a whale beached itself near Accra and died, Ghana's President Nkrumah and members of his cabinet left their offices and attended a funeral for it.

It is easy enough for us of the white nations, identifying our own reverential public rituals as rational, to look upon such an event as a prime example of primitive superstition. But not too long ago a ministerial colleague of mine was asked to "officiate" at the christening and launching of a new boat owned by a socially prominent Boston family.

A whale has special meaning to the coastal villagers of Ghana. Its vital force is that of a god of the sea, and its body must be enshrined with high honors. Not to do so is to run grave risks that its spirit will seek revenge against the local fishing fleets. Even if you do not believe, as Nkrumah most assuredly does not, that the spirit of a particular whale can play purposeful hob with the cause-and-effect relationships of fishing, there is still that mysterious and meaningful relationship of fisherman and sea, the *Nommo* relationship.

In the coastal traditions of Ghana, a dead whale is a very special kind of "thing." And man is the master of things through the productive or destructive power of the *word.* To bury a whale with suitable honors, and in the proper way, is, to an African, an eminently sensible method of giving good an advantage over evil. It was a special courtesy to their people that brought Nkrumah and his cabinet to the enshrinement of a whale.

With the broad African masses magic plays a crucial and continual role. Top African political leaders such as Nkrumah, Mboya of Kenya, Nyerere of Tanganyika, Luthuli of South Africa, Balewa of Nigeria, and Senghor of Senegal are more than able to hold their own in sophisticated company anywhere in the world; but this does not mean that they are out of touch with what goes on in the ordinary African mind. Nor should we be. Far from being on the wane, magic is enjoying a vigorous revival. The twin pressures upon Africans to remain traditional and to become modern are overwhelming, contradictory and unresolved. To traditional fears have been added a host of new ones, and there is no foreseeable outcome. This is a dismal state of affairs, one result of which is an intensified reliance on familiar magical practices. As white colonialism recedes, legal restrictions on magic weaken—sometimes as a result of deliberate policy in new black governments, sometimes because of a lack of interest in enforcement. One of the side-effects of Pan-Africanism is a heightened interest in *all* African traditional practices, including magic. Informed African observers of magic's resurgence still lay the heaviest stress on the all-pervading fear among ordinary people that a sure way to become a victim of evil magic is to repudiate or interfere with magical practices as such.

Frequently I found this fear at least faintly present in African intellectuals. There are relatively few members of the political elite who will come out flat-footedly against magic. In the present state of African affairs, a crusade by an African politician against magic would resemble in practical wisdom a crusade by an Alabama politician against "that old-time religion."

Robert Coughlan, the *Life* staff writer responsible for the article mentioned at the beginning of this chapter, called upon the vast network of news services available to his publication to pile up examples of African politicians responding to magic quite apart from how much of it they themselves may or may not believe. A cross-cultural equivalent, I suppose, is the way in which American presidents, just before and after election, become inveterate church attenders regardless of their previous records of indifference.

There is Albert Kalonji, self-styled "king" of the Congolese Balubas, whose eyes search the crowd for an albino woman whenever he returns from an official journey. Because Balubas believe that anyone who sights an albino will avoid bad luck, Kalonji's followers always make sure there is one available for him to see.

The ruler of Buganda was at one time exiled by the British colonial office. In protest, his courtiers let their beards grow. When he was finally permitted to return, the beards were ceremoniously shaved in public and the plan was to stuff a pillow with them for the royal throne. On sober reflection, however, it was realized that the ruler's political enemies might get hold of some of the whiskers and use them as part of a fatal charm against those who had grown them. Taking no risk, the shavings were destroyed.

Felix Houphouet-Boigny, the colorful president of the Ivory Coast and a former member of De Gaulle's cabinet, makes political capital of the "Houphouet" portion of his name. In his tribal language it has the singularly unattractive meaning of "cesspool," but its political merit is this: The president's maternal name is "Boigny" which he uses to honor his mother; "Houphouet" is a name given by his grandparents to their fifth child after losing four in infancy. It was a witch doctor who made the suggestion in order to confound the evil spirits responsible for the four previous deaths. He reasoned that a baby with such a disgusting name would not merit the spirits' concern. It worked, and the surviving child grew up to become the president's father. To keep the evil forces from discovering the trick and wreaking vengeance, the name is being passed down the line of generations.

The Central African Party is a moderate, multiracial political organization in the Rhodesias and Nyasaland. The organizing secretary of its Nyasaland branch was Bradford Phiri, who claims that he resigned because a curse was put on him by the followers of Dr. Hastings Banda. In his own words: "One day my nose began itching suddenly and a burning object moved from my nose to my left leg where it settled, causing me terrible pain which resulted in my being unable to walk. This illness was created magically by people who hate me."

Coughlan tells of a leading Ghanaian scholar and political opponent of Nkrumah who was frightened out of his homeland by a Ju Ju curse conjured against him by Nkrumah's henchmen. To strike a more pleasant note, I made the acquaintance of Ghana's former government minister, Mr. K. A. Gbedemah, a most delightful and urbane man. In our conversations about religion, he told me that he would describe himself as religious in a personal sense, but that he was too much of a freethinker to be comfortable in an orthodox Christian church or a Moslem mosque. "I start every day of my life with meditation," he said, "and I try to go through an entire day cultivating a spiritual sense. Three things I pray for: health to do my job, love in my heart, and a sense of God in my life. I hate no one. If someone disagrees with me, as many do, I try to let him go his own way, but with no hate."

At the time of our conversation, Gbedemah had a recently acquired Bentley automobile of which he was intensely fond. Before he set off on a trip with his chauffeur, his personal aides poured libations and performed other rituals over the car to assure a safe journey. Upon his return there was a more uproarious ceremony, including usually the sacrificial slaughter of a young goat in gratitude for the minister's safe trip. Traffic conditions being what they are in Ghana, there is a more compelling logic in this than might be supposed.

I asked Gbedemah how he felt about these practices. He said that he rather enjoyed pouring the libations himself, and was grateful enough for any efforts to assure his safety. He certainly took no exception to the intent of such rituals, nor was he prepared to argue against the belief of others in their possible effectiveness. The sacrifice of the goat he found personally distasteful, but again it was easy to respect the motivation.

It was difficult to tell exactly what Gbedemah did think about such traditional rites, but it was obvious that his free-thinking did not involve an iconoclastic crusade against the magico-religious practices of his people. Nor do I intend to imply that it should.

A few days before this conversation, however, I had met with Bishop Dagadu of the Ghana Methodist Church, and that dedicated man, now dead, told me that he could brook no compromise in his church's stand against the pouring of libations "as long as the act has religious significance and represents a belief that ancestors and Ju Ju spirits can actually intervene." I was visiting with Bishop Dagadu in the stucco meeting house where the quarterly session of the Accra Methodist circuit was being held, and I had just heard a long prayer by one of the lay delegates calling for divine guidance in the acquisition of a piece of property held by the government, but desired by the Methodists for a new chapel.

I wish now that I had discussed with Bishop Dagadu the fine points of intervention by ancestors and Ju Ju spirits as opposed to intervention by the Christian God through Jesus Christ. The questions were in my mind, but knowing of the Bishop's plans to visit Massachusetts in subsequent months, I felt that it would be more courteous to examine the matter in my study than in his. Unhappily, Bishop Dagadu did not live to make his American journey.

It is altogether too easy for modern Americans and Europeans to overlook the uses of magic in their own past and present, and to forget that, lacking other satisfying explanations and means of control, magic has a most appealing inner logic and spiritual authority. Its base is an instinctive reaction of man to the mysterious and often malignant behavior of the Nature of which he is a part. He sees the results of the activities of visible beings like himself. He assumes that activities he cannot understand stem from unseen beings, and from this he develops an entire spiritual universe.

The construction of such a spiritual universe has been long in the making in Africa and its foundations run deep. Africans, as we have noted, believe in a Supreme Being who created the cosmos. As Sékou Touré, the president of Guinea, explained when he was being quizzed about the possible slide of his country toward dialectical materialism, the existence of God is denied by dialectical materialism, but one would be hard put to find anyone in Africa, and particularly in Guinea, who does not believe in God.

But the Supreme Being, though heartily believed in, is not, in traditional African family and village life, necessarily worshipped. God is impersonal, distant, and at best a court of last resort. From God, however, streams the vital force which lodges in a vast created world of spirits. All of this was done originally in harmony, but the numberless forms of creation, receptacles of *Nommo,* frequently radiate their force in conflictful ways, disturbing the harmony of divine cosmos. This basic idea of power permeating the universe, possessed by men, animals, ancestors, gods, spirits, and things, makes life an arena of dynamic relationships between forces in which literally anything may happen. Religion thus becomes primarily ritual, the action of man through the *word* to keep power in balance and preserve the harmony of this vital cosmos.

Ritual action takes the forms we examined in connection with the Kalabari. The ancestral spirits and the spirit forces of destiny, Nature, village, and tribe are all involved; and obviously a man who can win these spirit powers and control them for the good of the tribe, or who can protect his kindred from evil spirits, is a great friend. But a Bantu youth padding along a path in his South African preserve is treading in the midst of a spiritual multitude of mixed hope and dread. The language of loathing would be all too tepid to describe his contempt and fear for the man or woman who is prepared to launch evil spirits against him, his family, or his tribe. Such a person, sorcerer or witch, is of enormous importance. He or she is the Achilles' heel of African life, the destroyer of harmony, the bringer of wicked curses, horrible diseases, and death. To tell an African believer that this spirit world does not exist, that a sorcerer's spells are nonsense, that witchcraft cannot bring on incurable diseases, is like telling him that fire does not burn. Africans are converted to Christianity, and they become convinced that the Christian God is *more powerful* than all sorcerers or witches. But as every missionary knows, African converts who *stop* believing in sorcerers and witches are few and far between. "Habit is a full-grown mountain; hard to get over or to pull down," says a Congo proverb.

Since it is through magic that the invisible forces are manipulated, there is need for the help of various specialists: priests or diviners who are in the service of particular gods; trance-mediums through whom the gods or spirits speak; soothsayers who answer difficult questions and foretell the future; and witch doctors, or good Ju Ju men, who are the individual's or the tribe's defense against sorcerers and witches.

The sorcerer, or Ju Ju man who specializes in black magic, has a number of ways of working evil. He is an expert in subtle poisons, which either kill, or, worse, drive people mad. He makes images and sticks pins into them, a technique called "the power of the doll." He is a master of hypnotism, and by the power of suggestion is capable of causing death. He can curse food that has been left over, or hair or nail clippings, and his act kills the owner of the article he has cursed.

He can point at a man with a conjured bone and slay him. There is no end to the frantic fascination in African folklore with a sorcerer's powers, but few whites who have lived in Africa for any length of time will deny that what Africans *call* sorcery and *believe* to be sorcery really "works." To such Africans sorcery is real and it is logical. There is no such thing as imaginary feeling about it. Sorcery is the ability to turn life's vital forces to evil ends. To doubt the possibility of this is to doubt the African's entire traditional conception of the spiritual universe. Everyone who has lived in Africa can tell his share of tales, awesome and ghoulish, of disasters and deaths which are simply unexplainable by normal medical or psychological techniques.

But if there is bad magic, there is also good magic. If the sorcerer is the public enemy, the witch doctor, as we shall see, is the defense against him and against his powers, just as he is also the defense against witches and witchcraft.

In Robert Coughlan's *Life* article there is a distortion which commonly appears in writings about African magic. Sorcery is confused with witchcraft. In Africa the two are clearly distinct. A sorcerer is a practitioner of conscious magic. He uses his spells and poisons knowingly and with premeditation. Moreover, he is usually a man.

Those who have read Joyce Cary's fascinating novel *The African Witch* will remember the skill with which Cary portrayed a woman who cast spells on her opponents and palsied a government. But except for being a female, this woman resembles no African witch. Witches in Africa are generally women, just as they were in Europe and Salem, but, unlike Cary's heroine, they are not public figures who work magic consciously for their own ends.

Witchcraft is still known in parts of Europe and America, but it has greatly died down from its salad days. In Africa it is deeply, actively—and perhaps even increasingly—in the tissue of everyday life. In the mental and social attitudes of Africans generally there is no belief more profoundly ingrained than that of the existence of witches. Witches are feared with a lively and ever-present terror. Passionate care is taken to avoid their activities. Many times, when I would put the question, I was told by educated Africans that they did indeed believe in witchcraft. Yet the answer was usually given with an edge of resentment, probably also of shame. In fact, the subject is a conversation-stopper, as between Africans and outsiders.

There are exceptions, of course, like the clerk in Ghana's health ministry, who told me: "Witches? Man, that's for the graybeards and the squares. In my crowd we dig Tom Paine, Einstein and Marx—mass action, technology and social significance!"

But witchcraft also has its social, or should we say antisocial, significance in Africa, and it is of the massive variety. It is hard to know, at the moment, just how witchcraft beliefs are to be measured against other important forces at work—education, modern medicine, scientific technology, churches—but this much is certain: The dense, complex web of change makes many of the old ways more rather than less tenacious. This seems to be as true in the overcrowded cities and towns as in the villages. Witchcraft rules African fears in realms where it counts, in all the treacherous shoals of strange disease, accident, inability to win promotions in office, mine, or shop, failure at school, disappointment in love, and lack of success generally.

Yet, as much as Africans fear witches, it is amazing how able they are to tolerate their presence, and to resist being stampeded into incessant witch hunts. Parrinder explains it this way: "Many people are believed to be witches, but as their powers are generally thought to be in abeyance they are not unduly disturbed. Only when there seems to be evidence that the witch is on the prowl... is action taken to restrain the witch's activities."

Dr. Wulf Sachs, in his exceptional psychoanalytic biography of a native African medicine man or witch doctor, *Black Anger*, recounts how John Chavafambira was first called upon to practice his arts. Warned by the spirit of his dead father that he was still too young to practice ("For the young to learn; for the mature to practice."), John allowed himself, nevertheless, to be drawn into a situation where he was expected to cleanse a bewitched kraal. For three years there had been no rain; the people were starving, the cattle dying.

Explaining to Dr. Sachs the impression the place made on him, John said: "The huts stood dirty and disorderly. They looked peculiar, they gave me a pain in the heart.... The little children were few, and they looked so dirty and without life. It was unusual, our kraals are always buzzing with babies.... I stood and looked at these poor, ill, unfortunate men and women, and I wondered if their troubles were due entirely to drought and starvation. Perhaps they prayed to the wrong god, maybe they were Christians and forgot the dead people."

But the kraal elder insisted pitiably that witchcraft was the cause, and that John, the strong, young Manyika doctor, was their last hope of smoking out the evil one who had bewitched them.

John found himself torn by indecision: "I felt sure that it was bad luck that had brought me to this bewitched kraal. Was I also in danger of being bewitched? But I had medicine in my calabash to protect me. I was thinking, should I disobey my father and help these unfortunate people?"

He agreed to do the smelling out, but, as we can see, it was no casual verdict, nor had the people of the kraal come lightly to their decision to identify the witch. Only the despair of their situation brought them to such an extreme move. Waves of witch-hunting do from time to time sweep across sections of Africa, but such occasions are exceptional.

Margaret J. Field, an extraordinary student of African life, says that even with the patient tutelage of the greatest witch-doctor-medicine-man in Ghana, it was some four and a half years before the subject of witchcraft crystallized in her mind into the shape in which she now sees it. This is the kind of reminder we of the West need of the complexity of the things we are called upon to understand in other parts of the world. Unfortunately, it is a type of humility found altogether too rarely in those missionaries, teachers, diplomats and technicians who go out "to work with the natives."

In what I am about to write on African witchcraft, I lean heavily on the insights of such people as Dr. Field, Evans-Pritchard, Parrinder and Meyer Fortes. Africans, to our loss, have not yet begun to write seriously about witchcraft, and, as I said, there is considerable embarrassment in their conversations about it. But a few Westerners have submitted to the disciplines and long years of personal involvement required for dependable observation and interpretation.

In the traditional witchologies of most African tribes, witches are usually women, just as sorcerers are usually men. The black art of witches is a bad "medicine," capable of acting destructively against other people. It is distinguished from sorcery in that there are no prescribed conjurings, incantations, ceremonies, or rites that a witch must perform. A witch projects her evil work directly from her mind, invisibly, and without ordinary cursing or invoking.

Witches behave as they do for no common reasons of hatred, jealousy, or spite. These emotions are natural and understandable in normal people, but witches are not normal people, and their wickedness is not a simple use of supernatural powers. Witches harm and kill the people it is *unnatural* for them to hate. In Dr. Field's words: "Ordinary bad medicine is found where one would expect to find it—among bad people. Witchcraft appears where one would not expect it—among good people. I do not mean that witchcraft works among the subtle undercurrents of jealousy and spite which run beneath the surface of every family and every social group and rarely ruffle the surface: that is where it would be natural to look for it. But the motives of the witch are felt to belong to a monstrous, sinister order of things that transcends comprehensible goodness and badness." (Shades of Neo-Orthodox theology!)

Our own Freudian revolution makes it easy for us to understand an assumption now commonly made about witchcraft, namely, that it is a medical phenomenon. Witches are emotionally or mentally ill. They are compulsively obsessed with the notion that they have the power to use their thoughts for harmful forays against others. With Dr. Field, I say that this medical thesis is not my business, "except in so far as it helps to convince the Europeans that the African point of view is based on a solid reality and not on a superstitious and senselessly cruel fantasy."

Much that can be said about witchcraft *is* convertible into Western psychiatric terms. An African told Dr. Field: "Witches often hide their witchcraft behind great kindness and gentleness. They seem to be very good, kind people all their lives and then at last when they are found out they confess that all the time they have been secretly killing people." Dr. Field found in Freud's *The Omnipotence of Thought* this fascinating, though ponderous, parallel: "A compulsion neurotic may be oppressed by a sense of guilt which is appropriate to a wholesale murderer, while at the same time he acts toward his fellow beings in a most considerate and scrupulous manner, a behaviour which he evinced since his childhood."

I dare say that many perceptive clergymen might recognize

in these words the razor's edge which separates them from those whom Africans call witches, and Freud calls compulsion neurotics.

What we have here is an interpretation of witchcraft on which the African and Western minds can agree: Witches are neurotics, eccentrics, whose *queerness* tips them over the edge, beyond the pale of normal mental controls and stabilizers. For most Africans the realm on the other side of "the edge" is sinister and terrifying. We should remind ourselves that it is only in recent years that we of the West have viewed it differently, and many of us have not even yet changed our viewpoint.

"Worked into this African system," says Dr. Field, ". . . are two additional classes of queer people who would also be recognized by Europeans as medical realities. First there are those obsessed with the fear that they are being bewitched, and, second, the still more terrified set of neurotics who believe themselves being made against their will into witches."

When we recall the intensity of disruption in current African life, the ferment of mobility, industrialization, uncertainty, and all the rest, it is by no means surprising that there is a swelling of the ranks of those who believe themselves to be witches, those who tremble at the possibility of being bewitched, and those who cower before the terror of booming witches. Africa's "Age of Anxiety" has a miasma at least as contagious as our own.

A striking feature of modern African witchcraft is the readiness and fluency with which witches confess once they are "smelled out" and confronted with their evil deeds. One is reminded at once of a similar phenomenon when witchcraft was thriving in Europe, and also of the kind of thing we have seen much more recently in the political trials of Soviet Russia and elsewhere.

Those deemed to be witches by the divination and ordeals

of expert witch-finders invariably let loose a torrent of detailed, ghoulish accounts of their wicked deeds. The setting for these macabre exploits is generally the same because there is much uniformity in African witchology. Witches leave their bodies asleep in their village huts or city homes, while they go winging off, usually naked, to nocturnal assemblies. Their coveys rarely consist of more than ten witches. Sometimes they fly as owls or other kinds of birds, and occasionally they ride upon the backs of animal "familiars," with which they work in close contact: leopards, snakes, black cats, and the like.

It is widely believed that witchcraft is hereditary, passed on from mother to daughter, but a girl child will normally show no signs of her blight until after puberty and child witches are rare. Then, too, while some are born witches, others may acquire the evil talent. Various beliefs prevail. Witchcraft may be purchased for a suitable sum. It may be obtained from demons or dead witches. It can be taken in with bewitched food. A witch can malevolently pass her witchcraft "substance" to unwitting recipients in numerous ways.

Always witchcraft is an activity of the soul or spirit, never of the physical body. When the *teme* of a witch goes off to an assembly, the body of the witch (back home asleep) will perish unless the *teme* returns.

At their nighttime carousings witches prey on other people. They procure the spiritual substance of their victims, sucking their blood and eating various parts of their bodies—always spiritually, of course, never in the actual flesh. What connection, if any, this may have with primordial memories of cannibalism is impossible to determine. It has no connection whatever, apparently, with the long-outlawed practice of ritual murder among a few African tribes.

But if the blood-sucking and body-feasting activities of

witches are purely nonmaterial, the physical results on victims are something else. Wasting diseases are believed to ravage victims' bodies, resulting eventually in death when some vital organ, such as the liver or heart, is spiritually devoured.

Gorging, however, is not the only activity of witches. Hardly less ominous are the wanderings of witches through the dreams of victims, foretelling nightmarish disasters and misfortunes for individuals, families, or tribes. And there is the casting of spells by sheer thought, the results of which are more than enough to harrow the bravest hearts.

Nowadays, since little can be done to witches in the way of physical punishment, their confessions have added therapeutic importance. Dr. Field's opportunities to hear and record such confessions among the Ga people were unique. Some of her material is well worth repeating:

> One witch, asked by the witch-doctor if all her own children were alive said, "Seven are dead. One remains alive."
>
> "What caused them to die?"
>
> "The members of our company [assembly of witches] have to make contributions in turn. When my turn came round from time to time I brought them to be killed by my company."
>
> Another said, "I killed Adwina Obronyi and I killed my five children."
>
> A male witch [there are some; Dr. Field's notes contain the names of seventy-three male and three hundred and sixty female witches] . . . said, "I have killed fifty people including my brother . . . and his son. Twelve out of the fifty were women."
>
> Another female witch said, "I have borne ten children, five are alive. I killed the others myself."

We must remind ourselves again that these are not physical murders, but killings of the essence—what Ga people call the *kla*—of a victim. The intent of the confession, however, is not the spinning of illusions. Physical death *has* occurred, and it is being explained.

Similarly, confessions of witchly cannibal feasts are not of physical eating, nor are they of physical assemblies. The witch's body remains on her bed. It is her "personality" that flies off to join other witches in gnawing on the souls of buttocks, thighs, heads, waists, and whatnots of victims. Still, the confessions have a terribly realistic quality, as witness:

> One woman, in confessing and repenting, said, "I am the mother of the child who is now sick. Our company have already shared the body. They gave me my daughter's heart to eat, but I did not eat it, and returned it to my daughter."

One of the most craven of crimes found in the confessions is that of causing barrenness. It is often considered to be worse than killing. A killed child can reappear in a future birth, but sterility deprives existing ancestors of their rightful reincarnation.

> One woman confessed that she had "taken the womb" of another and was asked by the witch-doctor, "How long have you had it?"
> "About a year."
> "Where have you put it?"
> "It is in an earthen pot in my house."
> "Will you let her have it back?"
> "I will give it back to her with joy."
> "Will you bless her as well?"
> "I will do so."

In such a case it would be crucially important that the stolen womb (or phallus in the case of a man) be the right one, and that it be unharmed, if "giving it back" is to have the desired healing effects. These details are very carefully considered in the cleansing of witches.

We need not go into numerous other forays of witches:

the causing of blindness and sores, inability to find a mate—in short, all kinds of misfortunes. In practice, however, witchcraft is often held responsible for such mundane matters as choleric dispositions, bad temper, and poor foo-foo. This is the intimacy of its connection with ordinary life.

It is when we come to the vital business of counteracting witchcraft that we begin to appreciate the stature and prestige of that much-maligned figure, the African witch doctor, medicine man, or *good* Ju Ju man. If the sorcerer and witch are the villain and villainess of the piece, the witch doctor is the hero, and he is so viewed in African life. Some of the most ludicrous mistakes of European administration in Africa have been made right here. The intent was understandable enough. Witchcraft is a source of great terror and fear. It is associated somehow with witch doctors. Truss up the witch doctors and maybe "this damn nonsense can be knocked out of the natives' heads!"

It is difficult to think of a comparable absurdity in our own culture, but it would be like fighting a crime wave by abolishing all law-enforcement agencies. Or, like attacking mental illness by outlawing the psychiatric and psychological professions. Blaming witch doctors for witchcraft is like blaming Jonas Salk for polio.

Yet the criminal codes of colonial administration have bristled with laws prescribing imprisonment for those who accuse or threaten to accuse persons of being witches or having the power of witchcraft. The purpose, obviously, was to protect innocent people from an African version of "McCarthyism." But from the point of view of Africans, who *believe* in the evil of witchcraft, and who, fancifully or not, actually *suffer* from witchcraft, nothing could be more muddleheaded than to punish the public benefactors who destroy it.

Reflection upon this may be helpful to those of us who have difficulty understanding the mental workings of certain

Americans. I have in mind the extreme anti-Communists, who are made furious by constitutional laws and principles which seem to protect those they are out to "expose." I mean no invidious comparison. It is the mental mechanism that interests me. If you believe strongly enough in the necessity of counteracting something (as most Africans do about witchcraft and some Americans do about domestic Communism), and if you believe that the "something" in question is a real, present and massive danger (as most Africans do about witchcraft and some Americans do about domestic Communism)—then it stands to reason that you can see only absurdity in restricting the witch doctor on the one hand, or the un-American activities investigators on the other.

We must understand that witchcraft is regarded by nearly everybody in Africa as a thoroughly evil and destructive force. The office of witch doctor, be he herbalist, diviner or priest, therefore is a worthy and honored one. I found this to be no less true in "detribalized" African cities and towns than in the heartland of old African tribal culture, the village.

One of the most remarkable things about witches is that their power is believed to be annihilated by the very act of exposing them. It takes, however, a person with a power stronger than that of a witch to unmask one; and it is thought that disaster will surely come to a weaker person who tries to expose a witch. Dr. Field writes: "The witch's townsmen . . . take her to the witch-finder only as a suspect. The actual accusation and exposure is left to him. Even he takes no risks, but follows up her exposure by making her perform a ceremony of renunciation and cleansing."

Putting witches to death has long been outlawed. As George Kahama, Tanganyika's Minister for Home Affairs, recently announced: "I must remind all that witchcraft is illegal for whatever purpose—such as removing other witches." So witches are not "removed." But it is not unusual for them to be fined and sometimes beaten—by their fellow-villagers, let me add, *not* by witch doctors. The humbling of a witch is a shattering social experience for the wretched person involved, and it is at this point that the witch doctor steps in as a curer of the soul. The prescriptions of witch doctors vary widely, but normally, include full confession, ritual cleansing, and rites for the healing of the witch's victims. The psychological climax is the pronouncement that the condemned and humiliated culprit is no longer a witch. The evil spirits in her soul are conquered!

Is it any wonder that the man who presides over these ceremonies of repentance and healing, the man whose powers are stronger than those of a witch's devils, is a giant in Zion?

Nor are the duties of this powerful figure limited to the curing of confessed witches. Turning to him also are those whose bones quake with the fear that they are *becoming* witches. Their nerves are hamstrung. Their bodies sicken. If anything, they are more difficult cases for the witch doctor's ministrations than those convinced of being out-and-out witches.

When such unfortunates turn to European doctors, or European-trained African doctors, they are frequently examined, told that there is nothing physically wrong with them, and sent home—only to grow steadily worse.

Dr. Field observed many cases of this kind and records some of the amazing cures wrought by witch doctors. She tells, for example, of a cocoa farmer who was "the picture of hunted wretchedness." His malady had begun with insomnia, interrupted by horrifying nightmares in which his soul was being dragged to an assembly of witches. His eyesight began to fail. His head rang with the voices of witches. His stomach was wracked with pain and scarred where cuts had been made to let out the sickness."

In despair he finally traveled by cocoa-lorry all the way to

Accra to see a European-trained doctor, who told him he could discover no organic illness.

When Dr. Field first saw him, the witches in his family had been exposed, and they had solemnly sworn to leave him alone. He was staying with the witch doctor and had recovered his sight.

Says Dr. Field: "... he was still wretched and weary, sitting about on the ground, afraid to go out of the sight of the witch-doctor. But in the presence of the witch-doctor he had a sense of safety and the belief that he was to be rescued. He stayed with the doctor about a year.... He gradually got fatter, lost his hunted look, and began to dare to go out alone. At the end he was a different creature, had developed a sense of fun, was chatty and quite energetic, and went home quite cured and confident of his power to remain so."

It is not surprising that after the depth of her experience Dr. Field testifies to her personal conviction that "a good witch-doctor *can* recognize a witch when he sees one and ... can tell when an illness is an ordinary one or one brought on by witchcraft. Translated into European idiom, he can tell when a person is a compulsion neurotic and an illness a functional or hysterical one. And he can and does cure."

That witch doctors are sometimes rascals and quacks is certain; as certain as that there are quacks and rascals in our own medical profession, to say nothing of the army of teacup readers, fortunetellers, mediums, yogis, phrenologists, and other assorted "healers" to whom thousands, yea, millions, of us flock "like sheep to be shorn." But it is just as certain that there are witch doctors who are no charlatans; who believe in their powers and their medicines; and who do indeed faithfully fulfill their function of cleansing witches, healing those who are in fear of becoming witches, and releasing from their pains those who believe themselves to be bewitched.

The training of a proper witch doctor is far from a casual matter, as Dr. Evans-Pritchard has so admirably demonstrated in his depth study of the Azande tribe. It consists of a rigorous apprenticeship, followed by an equally rigorous internship. His initiation into the ranks of his profession, as a fully trained practitioner, is no less solemn, though considerably more colorful, than the rites and red tape which attend a Western medical doctor's recognition as a licensed physician.

Nor is witchcraft his only concern. It is normal for Africans to regard *all* disease as having a spiritual cause, and to seek spiritual explanations and cures. Western-type hospitals and medical practices in Africa are widely criticized as cold and inhuman *because* they neglect this side of illness. Such attitudes are certainly not unknown in the West; but in Africa the very idea of healing suffering humanity is a spiritual idea, and the witch doctor is first and foremost a spiritual man.

In his study of the witch doctor John Chavafambira, psychiatrist Wulf Sachs speaks of John's amazing ability to reach and communicate with Africans confined in a Johannesburg mental hospital: "I must confess that by [his] method of approach he extracted from the insane a wealth of information far exceeding any that I did. Most of the patients not only submitted themselves to his interrogation, but regarded his efforts with confidence and trust. John, with his bones, horns, magical formulae and rituals, meant to them the real medical man. And I wonder if it wouldn't be advisable, from a psychological point of view, to employ *ngangas* [witch doctors] in the treatment of insane natives. In any case, there is nothing to lose, for our methods fail lamentably."

As I have said, European colonial governments vigorously legislated against witchcraft and witch doctors. In doing so they hounded and hindered the work of the witch doctor, thus earning the contempt and mockery of Africans, who, with independence, are now in a position to set their own patterns. What is the future of witchcraft and witch doctoring in the "new" Africa?

An inkling can be gleaned from an editorial which appeared recently in the *West African Pilot,* calling for the nationalization of witchcraft.

NATIONALISE WITCHCRAFT!

It is now time we nationalise witchcraft in Nigeria. We should do so with a view to putting a full stop to the perennial havoc being done to humanity since ages.

Let me say right here that witchcraft in the hands of civilised men is god-ordained but in the hands of the ignorant a bedevilled instrument. It is just like a scalpel (life-saving instrument) in the hands of a surgeon or a dagger in the hands of a lunatic.

It should be noted that in civilised countries as an agency of scientific promotion, witchcraft was being nationalised and national observatories were being built to promote research on it. That is why most civilised states big and small are being reckoned with as World Powers. We cannot become world power if we ignore this fact.

To make our independence worth the name I would suggest that a commission be set up forthwith by the Federal Government or any of its agencies, to take evidence in camera from the appropriate quarters for in this venture lies our hope for a national armoury.

The literary quality of this editorial leaves much to be desired, but what the editorialist is suggesting is worth examining. He is saying that witchcraft and activities to counter witchcraft serve a genuine purpose in African life. In fact, they serve purposes which in "civilised" countries are pursued through large-scale scientific research—in psychiatric centers, hospitals and laboratories ("observatories").

In Africa a tyranny of fear rules this realm, both because of the delusionary character of witchcraft and because of the occasional frauds practiced by some witch doctors and witch-finding agencies. But witchcraft keeps its grasp on men's minds because it operates in a spiritual sphere which Africans understand and believe in. In the colonial past there were no attempts to investigate and understand this (except by a handful of anthropologists). Governmental laws aimed at preventing unjust accusations against innocent people were decently motivated but misguided. They received no public consent and did little if anything to change beliefs in witchcraft. They treated symptoms and neglected causes.

Enlightenment is what is needed: understanding of the processes by which belief in magic and witchcraft develops, and of the ways in which the social malaises it mirrors may be treated with "a scalpel (life-saving instrument)."

Ways must be found to replace the dread underlying witchcraft with a new and enlightened kind of understanding. But this must be done in African terms and with full appreciation of deep-rooted African spiritual sanctions. Otherwise the unbalanced social conditions of modern African life are likely to strengthen rather than weaken the evils associated with witchcraft. An organized, sympathetic, scientific approach is called for—a "nationalised" approach.

This is neither the "tear it out root and branch" technique of colonial governments and Christian missions, nor the "leave it alone" advice of some anthropologists. Belief in witchcraft both produces and resolves the fears and tensions of African life. It is the fears and tensions which first require understanding, and, as our *West African Pilot* editorialist wisely proposes, this is a project of such huge proportions that nothing less than a "commission of the Federal Nigerian Government" is needed to begin the necessary work.

For all the patronizing nonsense that is written in Western newspapers and magazines about African witch doctoring, it is seldom that a Western physician who has worked extensively among Africans ridicules African remedies. Instead there is a growing appreciation of the obvious effectiveness of certain treatments by witch doctors. Pharmaceutical laboratories in America and Europe have been busy for some time analyzing various African medical plants sent home by impressed Western physicians and chemists.

The bitter conflict between missionary doctors and African witch doctors has been a popular theme for novels and short stories. The conflict, until recently, has been real enough; but lately there have been surprising efforts at reconciliation.

Diagnosis by a witch doctor is primarily a spiritual enterprise. For the Western physician it mainly is an attempt to identify tangible physical causes for which there is scientific proof. Along with this, however, has grown a general appreciation in Western medicine for psychosomatic ideas—the emotional, morale, and "soul" factors in illness. At the same time, witch doctors, no matter how grudgingly, are impressed by the successes of their Western counterparts. Gradually, and with little initial enthusiasm, the two groups have responded to a desire to learn from one another.

Many of the witch doctors' herbs are now under study, with scant results as yet in explaining their effectiveness. Among the most startling of these are plants administered to produce a flow of human milk. Dr. Kouadjo-Tiacoh, a European-trained African, wrote his doctoral dissertation on the witch doctors of West Africa. He describes how a maternal grandmother is expected to nurse an infant if the mother dies in childbirth. First she is placed on an opulent diet of honey porridge, kidneys, liver, goat udders, and testicles. At frequent intervals during the day she gorges herself on raw manioc, fresh peanuts, maize, and the seeds of cotton plants or papaya. Her breasts are just as regularly rubbed with these same plants.

In a remarkably short time the grandmother is ready to

nurse her grandchild! Contrary to usual African practice, however, the child is weaned as swiftly as possible—not because the milk dries up but because of the exorbitant cost of feeding the old woman.

Gone is the previous quick tendency of Western doctors to pooh-pooh the effectiveness of such "magical" milk-producing diets or rubs, and of depreciating countless other "symbolic" African cures. Little progress has been made in determining *why* African medicines work as they do, but the old smirking has been replaced by a humbler wait-and-see attitude. Dr. Pales of the Musée de l'Homme in Paris explains the changed approach this way: "In the past we used to analyze a plant used by the Africans and were unable to find any medicinal or nutritional value. For example, the analysis of manioc showed it to be very poor in food value. We concluded from this that the Africans used it widely because it was easy to grow. But then, when we decided to analyze it once more after steeping it in lukewarm water of the same temperatures as the branch channels of the African rivers, this steeping brought out food properties which had not even been hinted at by the first analysis. Analysis can be effective only if it exactly reproduces conditions in Africa. And as our methods of analysis are improved, we discover new properties in the plants we had hitherto scorned."

It is too much to expect that Western scientists who adopt an attitude of this kind toward African herbs will be equally open-minded about the curative qualities of sacrifices, magic spells, dances and incantations. There is simply too much tragic evidence of the failure of the witch doctors to conquer the ravages of leprosy, malaria, and sleeping sickness with their magic. But there is more than a germ of wisdom in Dr. Pales' words on reproducing African conditions in order to understand the healing properties of African medicines.

Those who scorn the spiritual basis of African life are

poorly equipped to reform either its witchcraft beliefs, or its medical practices. While African witch doctors are admitting to an ever greater extent that Western medicine is powerful and good, they remain highly suspicious of the ability of Western doctors to reckon properly with patients' souls. For some time to come in ordinary African life this concern with the soul will be expressed in the familiar traditional patterns of magic, sacrifice, exorcism, trances, witch-finding, and all the rest. But let us remember that these techniques, so odious in modern terms, are habitual and tested methods of placing the productive power of the *word* at man's disposal. *Nommo,* the life force, produces all life, all sickness, all health, all evil, all good, in the shape of the *word.* And since man has power over the *word,* it is he who may direct the life force. The influence of this outlook on assessing the causes and cures of life's disasters and diseases is rarely understood except by those who have been raised in a society that believes it. Sorcery, witchcraft, divination, and witch-doctoring are not hocus-pocus or mumbo-jumbo. They are Africa's traditional means of projecting a philosophy of life into an everyday coping with life. The traditional order is now in disarray, and in the long run most of its old practices are bound to go. What will remain—what *must* remain if the African soul is not to be destroyed—is the bedrock faith that man can control and direct the life force, either for good or for ill, and that through his power over the *word* he may fulfill life's meaning and purpose.

How this philosophy can be translated *out* of magic and witchcraft *into* something which both includes and transcends Western science is a great unexplored subject for research in Africa today, just as the *West African Pilot* editorialist said. The spirit that prompts explanation of evil, relief of suffering, and the consolation of human life is the

Prometheus stored now in Africa's desiccated calabashes of magic and superstition.

It was Montaigne who said: ". . . every man calls barbarism that to which he is not accustomed." Bronislaw Malinowski wrote: "Looking from . . . our high places of safety in developed civilization, it is easy to see all the crudity and irrelevance of magic."

Increasing numbers of Africans are themselves looking from "high places" at their past, and puzzling over the metaphysics of their emerging "new" societies. Assana Seck, a Senegalese and Lecturer in Georgraphy at the University of Dakar, has written: "Among the various underdeveloped areas, Black Africa was perhaps the one whose civilization was the least oriented toward an objective knowledge of the world and toward the acquiring of physical power. The Africans have left aside all attempts to discover physical laws and to domesticate matter; instead they have tried to discover *the spirit of each being and object in order to enable man to move about the world according to its inner rhythm* [italics mine]. This concept of the relations between man and the world surrounding him has resulted in a mode of existence which is so devoid of any dynamic principle that it is very near to mere equilibrium, though it has allowed the preservation of the black race and civilization in spite of its technical weakness. This lack of material power helps one to understand how easily colonization established itself in Africa."

In other words, the traditional African world was a stranger to our type of secular society, and an easy victim of its superior material power. Africa's concern with the "inner rhythm" of life, with "the spirit of each being and object," placed the highest possible premium on keeping things as static, as balanced, and as resistant to change as possible.

I remember the simple, poignant description by a Yoruba

chief, I. O. Delano, of the *iseku,* a ceremony for the dead among his people:

"The *iseku* ceremonies do not begin until late at night. The deceased may be an old man or a woman and age is determined by whether the deceased had a grandchild, or a marriageable child capable of performing ceremonies connected with his parent's funeral or not.

"A deceased person on his 'resurrection' or *iseku* day puts up an appearance of a happy man. This attitude is to convince the relatives that death is just a passage to a great hereafter. During the life time of an old person, those who will be responsible for the ceremonies connected with his funeral get many things ready. They practice quietly . . . the gait, movement and characteristics of the old man and the man who will act on the day of the deceased person's 'resurrection' usually moved close to him.

"On the *iseku* day the deceased man comes out in the dress in which he was popularly known when alive to convince the people that he was the dead man returned to earth for a few minutes to wind up his affairs. If the man personifying him had practiced well enough, he may present the deceased man so perfectly that the whole company bursts into tears on his appearance. He appears suddenly from an unexpected direction and those who have been waiting to meet him for the last time start an impromptu song of praise, reminding him of his good deeds whilst on earth. This occasion has before been a check on the life of many an old man when he remembers that a day of verdict will come when he will not be privileged to explain and the verdict may be a source of disgrace to his children. Songs on *iseku* ceremonies although they are worthy songs of praise could as well be songs of condemnation."

The net effect of the *iseku* ceremonies, so tenderly described by Chief Delano, is to preserve the equilibrium, the uninterrupted continuity, the changeless essence of a fixed and static way of life. No less than many others, the Chief now realizes that the old ways are responsible for Africa's lack of material power, lack of progress in science and technology, which in turn account for what Prime Minister Nehru has described as "the infinite tragedy of Africa during the past few centuries." Yet the Chief wistfully adds: "I believe Yoruba culture has many values which have been developed in the course of centuries. I would not like us to forget them or ignore them. Although many customs and traditions are out of date, there are certain basic characteristics which I think could make a definite contribution to human culture. I would like them not only to be kept, but to be put, at this time of our existence, in the forefront of our ambition for the future."

The Chief may not have had it in mind, but one product of Africa's ancient and passionate tryst with the supernatural has already spread as a revelation to the West—sculpture. As Matisse wandered from shop to shop in Montparnasse picking up fetishes for a few francs each, it never occurred to him that he was the "discoverer" of African art. He and the others—Picasso, Braque, Derain—loved the Ju Jus because they were an offense to conventional art; something to be waved about to taunt the worshippers of classical forms.

The precious genius of the African carvers—to these French rebels at least—was their scorn of realism. Here was beauty that cared not one whit for *reproducing* nature's forms. The African sculptors were truly creative; they were *free*, just as Gauguin, Cézanne and Van Gogh were free. Or so the rebels thought. Little did they realize that in one sense their "discovery" was better compared to the religious art of the Middle Ages than to modern "creative art." Still, African sculpture did help to revolutionize the art of two continents, and its Western devotees accomplished an ironical turnabout. The rumbles got back home and revealed to Africans for the first time that they *had* an art! It was startling news to an African carver to learn that he was an artist. Tribal societies knew nothing of art. This is a European conception, and language scholars who tried to work with the notion of "beauty" in tribal tongues found that it blends confusingly with words for goodness, fate or aptness. It was not beauty that the African carver was trying to create; it was communication with the spirits: to prevent them from doing evil, to win their benevolence and help, to keep *harmony* in the rhythms of life, to fend off the terrors of the unknown. What Westerners saw in a Bakongo statuette was a work of art. What the Bakongo sculptor saw was an object of worship. Every product of his hands and tools was part of his encompassing spiritual universe, a sacred object with a sacred role to play, a vessel of *Nommo*. From "our high places of safety in developed civilization" we look with awe at a Basonge mask from the Congo, and, if we are faithful to our accustomed categories, we must say that it is "the crudity and irrelevance of magic." For what the mask represented to the villager who carved it was the incarnation of "a terrible combat of supernatural forces."

When Chief Delano spoke of the man who personified the deceased at the *iseku* ceremony, he noted the realism of the performance. But the realism is symbolic rather than representational, as it is always in African sculpture. We need a descriptive label, so we say that African art is "expressionistic." To embody the spirit of the Dead, there is no need for the *iseku* stand-in, or an African carver, to reproduce a dead man's features. At the *iseku,* particular attributes are stressed—clothing, gait—and in a mask it might be any dominant characteristic—the nose, the lips. But the rest need bear no resemblance to human form. There is no waste, no embellishment. The sacred purpose is to evoke only the essence, the vital force, the innermost rhythm.

There is something else in African art, however, which has a subtle appeal to Westerners smothered by their asphalt and steel cities: its earthiness and sensuality. When drummers and tom-tom players begin to pound their instruments, the blood flowing in human veins responds with a rhythm of its own. The feet of dancers pounding the earth stir more than dust. African sculpture embodies somehow this same earthiness, not only in its forms and materials, but in physical participation. African artists are not a small, set-apart class serving a spectator public. Professor Marcel Griaule notes in his study of African art that craftsmanship is a part of tribal life "no one would dream of avoiding." Just as a man hunts so, too, does he carve, paint, decorate, dance, and play a musical instrument. Some are better than others, of course. Villages are proud of their "best" dancers, drummers, storytellers or sculptors, but it is a matter of degree not of separateness. The "singer" back at Awo Omamma was described to me as "the best in all of Ibo land"; but his eminence did *not* stem from originality. Nor does it do so in any of the traditional African arts. And there's the rub. There have been no artistic honors in old African life for originality. Instead the aim has been to preserve faithfully and exactly the ways of the past.

So, while the discovery of African art has given a precious gift of creative freedom to the West, it must be judged on its own soil as still another piece of a stagnant world. Through its ministering magic, a race and a civilization have been helped to survive. But now among the survivors are rapidly growing numbers of tormented and aspiring men. They look about and see everywhere that the old "sacred" world of Africa is dying and a new "secular" world is struggling to be born. The old world is found wanting for the development of the new "African personality." And one of the strangest features of the fate of African religious art is that religious proselytizing struck it a mortal blow. Except in some of the most isolated and off-the-beaten-track areas, traditional African art is in decay because it was *not* secular. Its inspiration depended upon a closed supernatural system in which there was no room or need for alternatives; and into that closed system came idol-smashing Islam, and a Christianity with no patience whatever for "heathen" practices. Wherever seeds of doubt about the gods have been sown, the spark has gone out of African artistic expression. Among our old friends, the Kalabari, for example, many men now content themselves with contributing money for the home village ceremonials which priests (or their substitutes!) can use to make offerings to the gods while they themselves stay at their city jobs or out in distant fishing camps.

But it is not only Christianity and Islam that bear the burden of reducing the old sacred arts to tourist industries. There is far more to it, for the temptation has been overwhelming to bow slavishly to the material power of the white man's world. As Thomas Diop has written: "There is no need to go into detail as to the horrors of this prolonged servitude. . . . This tragedy entailed a long eclipse of the African personality and reduced the African to the status of an inferior man, a man scorned." How does it happen then that Africa, in a few short years, has made such giant strides toward freedom? Diop answers: "Africa began to learn new lessons in the harsh school of life, she rediscovered her deeper personality and attempted to reshape it in order to meet the demands of life as she saw it through her painful experience."

There has in fact been a "rhythm" in Africa's tragic spiritual journey through servitude. In Diop's words:

> Constantly reflecting upon her own fate, Africa realised that the reason why she had fallen victim, at a particular moment in her history, to a superior technique of destroying human lives was that during the first stage of her rather solitary evolution she had never imagined that there could be any reason for developing the art of killing and destroying to such a point of perfection, even if only for the purpose of ensuring one's own security.
>
> Pursuing their meditation on the nature and aspects of the infinite tragedy of Africa, successive generations of Africans perceived that spiritual servitude is the worst servitude of all, and that it leads to the stifling of all personality. The African personality has since attempted to extricate itself from the chaotic mass of racial prejudice in which it was caught. Just as human experience is unending, so the personality develops uninterruptedly; it is unswervingly directed towards fulfillment of Africa's finest possibilities.

So more and more the reflective African has come to feel that his culture's extravagant concern with the spirit world has stifled development in areas of material progress—technology, science, and, above all, the power to assert sovereignty. In this there is universal agreement among African leaders. They yearn to diminish—and rapidly—the excessive dependence of African societies on the *static* world of spirits in which the ordinary African has attempted to discover life.

Yet these same leaders will insist that the traditional African view of vitality in life, of some force which endows all beings with meaning and purpose, must be preserved. How else could there be any hope of discovering Africa's deeper personality? How, the African thinker asks, has the culture of Africa managed to survive at all in the face of the catastrophic assaults made upon it? What has made the survival of African societies possible in spite of their obsession with equilibrium and their overwhelming material weakness? How has the black race, despite its humiliation, been able to endure, not only in Africa, but also throughout the "New World"?

Many of Africa's intellectuals now believe that to find the answers to these questions, to unravel the mystery of the black race's endurance, to explain the persistence of black cultures and societies in spite of crushing abasements, would clarify the meaning and relevance of traditional African spiritual views for the emerging, free African nations.

Some have suggested that the mystery of African survival must be credited to a "transcendental intelligence." Indeed, many believe that such a faith is utterly essential if Africa is now to arrive at a synthesis, a new synthesis, of her own life with the materialisms of both the East and West, *without losing her soul.* They claim that the harmony between man and Nature, between man and the realm of spirit, has not only characterized traditional African society but must remain the vital force and underlying principle of new African societies as well.

Léopold Sédar Senghor, President of Senegal, is one among many to explore the mysteries of rhythm in this respect, and he has written:

> What is rhythm? It is the architecture of being, the internal dynamism which gives it form. The system of waves which emits to the attention of others, the pure expression of the vital force. Rhythm, it is the vibratory shock, the force which, through the senses, seizes us at the roots of being.
>
> It is by the rhythmic incantation of the word that the sorcerer invokes the vital force. What is indicated here is the participation in the cosmic essence through sensuality, in its unvulgarized, essential meaning, in contrast to the contemplative tradition of the Orient and the West.

The American Negro writer, Samuel Allen, has noted Senghor's insight into the contrasts present in tribal dancing —how the lesser members of a dance group become enveloped in sensual agitation while simultaneously the head dancer is participating in the serene beauty of the masks of the Dead. And he goes on the say:

> The vibratory effect of the spoken word, accompanied as it is in Africa, by the percussion instruments, achieves a communal participation in the vital force or universal essence, recalling in contrast the more individualistic and contemplative visions of the English poets, Blake and Vaughan. It was an African, curiously, who, several centuries earlier, viewed religious contemplation as a group affair and who was impressed by the rhythmic sequence of the word of God. "Out of silence," said the Bishop of Hippo (St. Augustine), "came the voice of God; the first word, the second, and the third, and so forth, until the penultimate word, and the last, and the silence."

If the total commitment of traditional African societies to the *teme* world has had its drawbacks, it has also had—in the profound spiritual significance of rhythm, for instance—its virtues.

Thoughtful Africans look hard at the rigors of rationalism and the mechanistic world view, and they see that here, too, are both virtues and vices. The imminent questions for them are these: How can the *élan* of traditional African religious views, the belief in the creative intelligence of both the seen and unseen worlds, be preserved, while the ugly terrors and suffocating conservatism are cut away? What are the elements out of the spiritual past which should be projected into the new African societies? Above all, how can Africa arrive at a new synthesis of man and God, man and Nature, man and man?

These questions, as an African friend says, are "most problematic." Upon the answers, however, depends much of the future of the new Africa. A tremendous contest for African souls is under way. It is wise for us to see in this contest what Malinowski calls "the embodiment of the sublime folly of hope, which has yet been the best school of man's character."

IV

Allah in Africa

DEAR listeners, Assalamo alaikum. Although it seems a little late, I think it is not very much out of place for me to extend my hearty Id [holiday] greetings to all of you who are listening and to your families and friends. I say Id Mubarak and I pray to God that He may shower His blessings on all of us. Amen.

"And now I come to the questions. The first question comes from Mr. R. Olajide Bakare of 10 Bankole Street, Lagos. . . ."

The pleasant, authoritative voice speaking these words belongs to Maulvi Naseem Saifi, Chief Ahmadiyya Imam, and spokesman for a program called "Islamic Point of View" which is broadcast Monday evenings on Radio Lagos of the Nigerian Broadcasting Corporation.

Each day of the month at least two Moslem programs are heard; on Mondays and Fridays there are usually one or two more. Presiding over this vigorous enterprise of mass-media evangelism is Alhaji M. K. Ekemode, who organizes in any single week programs covering such diverse topics as "Islamic Mode of Worship," "Islam and Students," "Islam on Physical Development," "Islam—the Religion of Peace," and "The

Holy Koran—A Standing Miracle." Some of these programs are in Yoruba, some in Hausa, and some in English. To the microphones of Africa's NBC, Alhaji Ekemode brings the top preachers, Imams, and intellectual leaders of Nigeria's Moslem community. There are fairly vitriolic "denominational" cleavages among the Moslem faithful, but Mr. Ekemode rallies all factions to his cause—the cause of spreading in West Africa the faith which proclaims, as he puts it, "salvation based on good deeds rather than dogma." He confidently expects Islam to become the national religion of Nigeria, and eventually of all Africa, partly because "its make-up is so simple, so adaptable, so practical."

To see how simple, adaptable, and practical a face Islam exhibits to a Nigerian radio audience, let us return to Maulvi Naseem Saifi, who, incidentally, was the unrequited challenger of Billy Graham during the famous evangelist's Lagos crusade. He was about to take up a question from Mr. R. Olajide Bakare, who asked about the significance of ritual blessings called Naflas, usually said either before or just after certain daily prayers, Mr. Saifi answered:

> Naflas means something more than what is obligatory. We read in Holy Koran: "Observe Prayer at the declining and falling of the sun to the darkness of the night and the recitation of the Holy Koran in Prayer at dawn. Verily the recitation of the Holy Koran at dawn is specially acceptable to God. And wake up for it in the latter part of the night as a superogatory service for thee. It may be that thy Lord will raise thee to an exalted position."
>
> In fact the real love for doing a thing can be known only when a person does a little more than what is obligatory. What is obligatory, he must do and he cannot avoid it. So when he does only that much it cannot be said that he really likes it. But when he does a little more then his real mind is known and it can be rightly said that he is doing it willingly. It is this kind of thing

that brings great reward. In fact it is only this kind of thing that puts one man in a more exalted position than others. The Naflas that people observe before or after prayer, and specially in the latter part of the night, are a means of receiving blessings of God. They bring us very much nearer to our Creator.

I should like to advise all the Muslim Brothers and Sisters to pay great attention to Naflas and during the Naflas they should pray for the spread of Islam and unity and solidarity of the Muslims all over the world. May God bless you all. Amen.

This is a simple, personal, homiletic approach. But what about the "practical" side of Islam's message? Saifi's next question is from a Mr. Aribiyi Maiyegun of 3 Ikoyi Road, Lagos, and he asks: "I started fasting at the age of ten. But at a certain stage in my life I was seriously ill, with the result that since my recovery, it has never at any time been possible for me to fast throughout the month of Ramadan. What do you think is the remedy for my present condition, bearing in mind that I am regular in prayer?"

Dear Mr. Maiyegun, as you will now realize you made a great mistake by fasting at the age of ten. The age of ten is a tender one and great harm can be done to one's physique by keeping fasts. That is why our religion which is very practical forbids children to fast. You might have heard me quite often advising the parents not to allow their young children to fast. However now that you have already done harm to your physique, my only suggestion is that you must take care of your health and try to regain the lost vitality. Till you are normally strong, as strong as a man of your age should be, or as you would have been if you had not done any harm to your health, I should like to advise you not to fast. But please do not remain contented in your present position. Consult a doctor and treat yourself well. I am sure with the grace of God you will become strong enough to fast again. And will you write to me next year again to tell me what your position is. I shall be very much pleased to know that you have regained your full health.

Eminently practical. Even more, *intimately* practical. But what of adaptability? Here next is a question from Mr. P. O. Ajanaku (it is worth passing notice that not a single query is from a woman), asking: "You said in one of your answers to a certain question that a Muslim should not take part in the burial ceremony of his pagan relative. Suppose a pagan parent dies in a compound where all members of his family are Moslems, what does Islam say about such a situation? Should he be buried without washing or, if not, what is to be done before he can be buried?"

Not at all, my dear Mr. Ajanaku. Why should he be buried without washing? What Islam forbids is taking part in pagan *ceremonies*. The dead body, whosoever it may be, must be given due respect. The Holy Prophet used to stand up for respect when the funeral procession of a Jew or a Christian or even a pagan passed by him. It is not the man himself or his dead body that we hate and avoid. It is the paganish customs. This pagan parent that you are talking of should be given a good washing and buried properly.

But one thing, I must confess, I do not understand. Is this pagan you are talking of the last pagan in the world that no other pagan is available to wash him and bury him?

Please remember Allah has said in the Holy Koran that the Holy Prophet is a Mercy for the worlds. We who are the followers of the Holy Prophet should also prove ourselves to be a mercy for the world. The touch of human sympathy must never be lost. It must always be applied everywhere and to everyone. The greatest sympathy that can ever be needed is at the time when someone dies. Do show sympathy and do not turn away from the people with a stiff neck. O God help us show to the world that we are real followers of the Holy Prophet who is a mercy for the world.

This indeed is adaptability, but of a quite different kind than that described by many Christian missionaries to their home congregations in Europe or the United States. What is usually stressed in such reports is that Islam adapts, for the sake of conversions, to virtually anything in African life. The "easy morality of Islam" is a favorite phrase. I have read a dozen or more book-length reports of experienced Christian missionaries in Africa, representing a broad denominational cross-section. There are a few notable exceptions, but the great bulk content themselves with a comparison of the best in Christianity with the worst in Islam. This is no way to educate Western public opinion on the current role of Islam in African life. There are Moslem high roads and there are Moslem low roads in Africa today, and over both are passing throngs of black faces.

Leaving aside North Africa and Egypt—countries almost entirely Moslem—and concentrating on sections of sub-Saharan Africa where Christianity and Islam compete, we find these recent estimates of Moslem affiliation:

Country or Groups of Countries	Population base: 100	% Moslem
(former) French Equatorial Africa	100	30% of total pop.
(former) French West Africa	100	34% " " "
(former) British Cameroons	100	50% " " "
Gambia	100	84% " " "
Liberia	100	20% " " "
Nigeria	100	33% " " "
Nyasaland	100	9% " " "
Sierra Leone	100	11% " " "
Tanganyika	100	19% " " "

The Christian God and the Moslem Allah are offered to the emergent continent of Africa in a maelstrom of changing social patterns, and Africans are judging afresh the spiritual systems which have so deeply influenced the life of mankind. Neither Christianity nor Islam is a newcomer to Africa, but the situations they face today are new in depth and breadth. Weakened by the decay of traditional social structures, the tribal religions are losing force. Centered as they are in single villages or tribal areas, with no strong sanctions beyond these limits, they are no longer capable of commanding the loyalties or aspirations of a growing number of Africans, who, in turn, are attracted by more universal spiritual fare. On the one hand, there is a yearning for the status, the significance, and the challenge of the great monotheistic world religions; on the other hand, there is a profound desire to preserve the historic spiritual values of African society.

Islam, as a major protagonist in this drama, has a heritage of thirteen centuries of association with certain areas of Africa, and today it is showing ever-greater missionary concern. In Africa, with an estimated population of 220,000,000, there are some 81,000,000 Moslems north of the Sahara, and perhaps as many as 31,000,000 south of the Sahara. The latter are to a considerable extent concentrated in a broad belt extending from Dakar and the Republics of Senegal, Mali, and Guinea along the northern areas of all the countries of West Africa and especially Nigeria, across the Republics of Chad and the Congo, to Kenya, Ethiopia, Somalia, Tanganyika and the shores of the Indian Ocean.

This is the base from which Moslem traders, missionaries and teachers proclaim in widening circles that while Islam is a "religion of the dark-skinned," it is also one great universal brotherhood open to all races and peoples, and summoning them to acknowledge that "there is no god save God [Allah] and Mohammed is His Prophet."

History brought Islam to Africa in three waves. In the year of the Hegira (A.D. 622), Mohammed took time out from the immediate matter of his flight from Mecca to Medina to send some of his persecuted followers to Abyssinia, sustaining their drooping spirits with the promise that Islam would soon show its signs in the remotest regions, "until it will become quite clear . . . that it is the truth." Within ten years after the Prophet's death (A.D. 632) Islam was invading Egypt in force. During the years 661-750 the Moslem conquest extended across North Africa and into the Sudan. From the eighth to the thirteenth centuries it struck southward and established cultural sway over the powerful successive African empires of Ghana, Songhai and Mali. Only the malignant tsetse fly seems to have stemmed further advance through the savannahs and rain forests to the south.

Meanwhile, a second wave flowed down the shores of the Red Sea and the Indian Ocean. By the fourteenth century there were citadels of Islam strung along Africa's lush east coast; thriving communities of merchants, seamen, and caravan companies trading in ivory, spices, gums, slaves, and gold.

The third wave dates from about 1750 to the beginning of the present century, during which time a missionary fervor was aroused by the Sufi orders in response to the evangelical efforts of Roman Catholics and Protestants, who came first from Europe and later from North America.

During these various periods, Islam penetrated Africa with shrewd combinations of four principal techniques: (1) conquest through "holy war"; (2) the commercial influence of merchants and traders; (3) peaceful missionary propaganda by the followers of Sufi orders and by graduates of Islamic schools in Cairo, Fez, and Zaitouna; and (4) the intermarriage of Moslem traders and religious leaders with African women.

Dr. Tracy Strong, Visiting Professor of Missions of the Federated Theological Faculty of the University of Chicago, has put together an excellent summary of Islam's present posture in various segments of Africa. I follow his basic outline:

Egypt and the Sudan

Cairo, seeking ever-closer links with tropical Africa, is energetically emphasizing the need for Islamic unity through regular radio broadcasts, the dispatch of large cadres of Al-Azhar-trained missionaries, and the summoning of frequent conferences of African Moslem scholars and spokesmen. African nationalism is encouraged by the Egyptian Moslem religious leadership no less than by Egyptian Moslem political leadership.

The Sudan—with its 6,350,000 Moslems, 3,500,000 tribal religionists, and 400,000 Christians—is a turbulent area of religious ferment. The Northern Sudanese, who received Islam enthusiastically enough, exercised their genius for assimilation by molding the religion of the Prophet to their own tastes rather than to the likes of theologians. As Strong says: "They sang in it, danced in it, wept in it, brought their own customs, their own festivals into it, paganized it a good deal, but always kept the vivid reality of its inherent unity under the rule of one God." The tribesmen of the Southern Provinces, meanwhile, have clung doggedly for the most part to their traditional religious life, resisting Moslem *and* Christian missionaries with fine impartiality. Such Christian converts as there are have received more education and provide the bulk of political leadership.

Ethiopia, Kenya, and Tanganyika

Emperor Menelik once called Ethiopia "an island of Christians in a sea of Moslems," and the Glasgow scholar, J. S. Trimmingham, calls attention to the delicate situation of both Christian and Islamic missions because of the existence in Ethiopia of a unique and ancient African State Church. But Ethiopia has a long history of relations with Islam, and many of her people retain an intriguing combination of pagan and Islamic ties. Performance of Moslem prayers, observance of Ramadan, and pointing of graves toward Mecca mingle with the familiar paraphernalia of traditional tribal practices in a strange and chaotic pattern.

One of the oldest and most vigorous Moslem groups is the Arab-Swahili community along the coastal areas of Kenya and Tanganyika. The Arab forefathers of this mixed and prosperous brotherhood were pioneer explorers of East Africa. There are many old, aristocratic, and wealthy families, who, like some of their New England counterparts, have built upon fortunes first made in the slave trade. The Arab-Swahilis support Islamic missionary enterprise but of a genteel and tolerant sort.

Centered in Nairobi, amidst symbols of culture, affluence, and humanitarianism, is the close-knit Moslem Ismaili Khojas community, whose spiritual and temporal leader is the young, Harvard-educated Aga Khan V.

The Aga Khan has very modern ideas about leading his flock in the atomic age, and his followers, made up mostly of Indians, are one of Africa's wealthiest and most progressive sects.

The strongest Moslem missionary impulses in East Africa stem from the Ahmadiyyas with headquarters in Kenya. Because of the vigor of this wide-ranging program we shall say more about it in another context.

The Rhodesias, Republic of South Africa, Republic of the Congo, Republics of Former French Equatorial Africa, and the Cameroons

There are stepped-up Moslem missionary activities in the Rhodesias, but the total number of Moslems is still comparatively small. Many of the men who come to Northern

Rhodesia from Nyasaland and Ruanda-Urundi to work in the copper mines bring their Islamic faith with them. The capital, Lusaka, has an attractive new mosque that was pointed out to me, very proudly, by an African driver of the British South Africa Company.

Peter Mathews of the Mindolo Ecumenical Center, an extraordinary enterprise of which we will speak later, told me that Islam was spreading much more rapidly than many Christians suspected and "should be taken seriously."

In Southern Rhodesia more than 120,000 Moslem workers from Nyasaland have built a network of mosques and communities. As yet they have little contact with a tightly organized community of Indian Moslems, which has gotten up a fine head of steam for modernizing Islam's educational approach to youth. One of the leaders told Tracy Strong that his group sees Islam "as the greatest unifying force in our lives where we are a minority Indian group in a struggle for power by the African and European communities."

Beautiful Durban holds one of South Africa's strongest Moslem communities, again largely made up of Indians, but in Johannesburg, many African migrant workers from Mozambique and the north are Moslems. In Cape Town there is an ancient Moslem community, the Malays ("coloureds" in South Africa's bizarre racial terminology), and Islam is the force which holds this beleaguered group together. Whenever possible young Malays are sent to Egypt, Pakistan, and other Moslem countries for higher education.

Few Moslems are to be found in the Leopoldville and the western areas of the Republic of the Congo, but elsewhere in this vast new independent state there are pockets of tribal groups with long-standing Islamic loyalties. Leaders of these tribes are frequently sent to Tanganyika for training in Moslem schools.

In the string of Republics punctuating what was formerly

French Equatorial Africa there are relatively few Moslems. Chad is a major exception, its population being seventy-eight per cent Islamic.

The Cameroons are a chaos of contending religious forces, with Moslems and Christians stepping up their activities intensively. Many of the leaders are secular-minded, tribal loyalties remain strong, and the Christian churches have unusually vigorous African spokesmen. In the north, where the chieftaincy is still a powerful institution, Islam is especially robust.

Dahomey and Senegal

While it is estimated that only seventeen per cent of Dahomey's population is Moslem, there are signs of a powerful missionary thrust among the Yorubas in the east. Mosques are appearing—seven in the last few years. Tribal life is hardy, however, and Islam seems more like a surface covering than a deep, inner penetration.

In Senegal's bustling port of Dakar, about ninety per cent of the population is believed to be Moslem, and itinerant missionaries have broadened Islam's influence in village areas as well. There seems to be an unusually strong consolidation of Islamic and traditional religious practices here. The newly independent government is not anxious to encourage Christian missionary work. In fact, the situation is discouraging enough to stimulate Roman Catholics and Protestants to talk gingerly of making common cause.

Guinea, Sierra Leone, and Liberia

Sékou Touré, the ambitious and able president of Guinea, is no enthusiast for religious proselytizing. His country is predominantly Moslem, and he has recently been to Mecca as befitting the leader of such a country; but he is an advocate of secular socialism, and for a while it appeared that an antireligious educational campaign might be launched. Plans were dropped before they materialized. The widely held notion that Guinea is a "Communist" country is premature to say the least. Marxist principles of political organization are vigorously applied. Most youth activities have been taken out of the hands of religious groups and turned over to the state. But Touré makes it abundantly clear that his base is African nationalism, not Soviet-Sino Communism. He emphasizes, as mentioned previously, that it would be extremely difficult to find anybody in Guinea who does not believe in God. And in Guinea the ascendent designation for God is Allah; His dominant prophet is Mohammed.

Tiny Sierra Leone numbers 588,000 Moslems among its 2,350,000 people, and 70,000 Christians. Most of the rest maintain the old customs and beliefs. Typical of West Africa in general, one is likely to find a miscellany of religions in a single family or village. The atmosphere is tolerant, and religious affiliation is not a focus for strong feelings. J. Spencer Trimmingham, writing of the catholicity of Moslem chiefs, says: "They keep up the ancestral cults. They support Islam to the extent of becoming adherents, and they encourage Christian missions out of appreciation of their education and social welfare, attending church services as they also honour Islamic festivals. The three religions each fulfill a social function, and since adherents are all found in each chieftaincy all are accorded recognition." Activities of the Ahmadiyya Mission are spirited. It has helped to build some twenty-five mosques, and it has an agile corps of young missionaries "devoting themselves to the spiritual and educational progress of the land."

Liberia, with a population of 1,500,000, estimates that there are only about 100,000 Moslems and 200,000 Christians in the land. The rest retain ancestral loyalties. The Islamic communities are concentrated in the north. In Monrovia there is a mosque, and the government recognizes Moslem holidays, as do virtually all governments in West Africa. No attempts are made to curb missionary work, and the Ahmadiyyas, who came to Liberia only in 1957, are fanning out to make converts.

Ghana and Nigeria

The Republican Constitution of Ghana, which became effective on July 1, 1960, provides that "no person shall be deprived of freedom of religion." The country has a population of about 5,000,000, of which perhaps 1,500,000 can be reckoned as either Moslem or Christian. The Christian count would be about two-thirds of this total. There is a long history of resistance in Ghana to Moslem pressures, a resistance rooted in the ancestral faiths; but by 1932 a Moslem Association was founded as a cultural organization to foster Islamic unity and seek reforms giving greater recognition to Islam in the legal and educational systems. It entered politics for the first time in 1939 by backing candidates in the Accra municipal elections. By the 1954 general elections the Moslem Association Party was claiming wide support in the Colony and Ashanti, but of its sixteen candidates only one was elected. The formation of the M.A.P. brought a strong reaction from Dr. Nkrumah and his Convention Peoples Party. Nkrumah opposes the introduction of religion into politics; and to head off any further Moslem excursions into politics, the C.P.P. set up an internal Moslem Council to consider proposals for establishing Koran schools, for introducing the Koran into government schools for Moslem pupils, and for sponsoring a C.P.P. Imam in Accra. This gambit seemed to work. In the 1956 elections the M.A.P. put up only three candidates; again one was elected.

In the Northern Territories, Moslems did not attempt to

organize politically, but a good deal of Moslem support was given to the Northern Peoples Party. Of the 104 seats in the 1954 National Assembly, fifteen were held by Moslems (including two Ahmadis). This is roughly equivalent to Moslem numerical strength relative to the population as a whole. The situation has remained pretty much the same except for the increasingly energetic activities of the Ahmadiyya movement. Since Ghana's independence in 1957 the Ahmadiyyas have built between 150 and 200 mosques and established many schools. Ghana's smartly trained army has Moslem chaplains, which creates certain tensions when both Christians and Moslems are ordered to officiate at ceremonies such as the dedication of a soldiers' memorial.

In 1959 a special conference of Christian pastors was convened at the University to mull over the relationship between Moslems and Christians. The pastors very creditably agreed that it could be highly valuable for Christians and Moslems to meet, converse, and try to understand one another in an atmosphere of friendliness and mutual respect. Their report stated:

> If Muslims know anything about Christian theology they tend to think that the doctrine of the Trinity is the teaching about three gods. The theological questions are important but they do not bulk large in the actual social, moral and ethical issues. Islam spreads through the way its festivals are celebrated. The celebrations take place in the home, not the mosque. They become an affair for the neighboring people who are attracted by the beauty, color, music, dancing and simplicity which characterize their celebrations. People come to witness and are attracted to the religion. It is said by the Muslims that Christianity holds up an impossible ideal of the relations between men and women. In Islam a different standard is set up and the average man can attain it. Again it is said that Christianity sets its face against anything that is remotely pagan so that it tends to destroy much of the indige-

nous way of life; its converts drift into the rootless cosmopolitan ways of the West. The Muslim proselytiser comes as one African to another, and leaves his convert still rooted in his indigenous way of life and yet introduces him to a world-wide brotherhood.

Dr. Noel King, for many years a Christian theologian at what is now the University of Ghana, expects Islam to run up impressive gains in Ghana in the next several years. He told me how impatient he becomes with the "patronizing" attitude of Christians toward Islam. "Too few Christian theoreticians," he said, "seem to take into account the tremendous emotional impact upon a man when he goes to pray with his fellow Moslems. At that moment he becomes truly a man, the equal of any man, a brother in a vast brotherhood. He walks away from prayer certain of his worth, come what may."

Sir Abubakar Tafawa Balewa, first Prime Minister of the Federation of Nigeria, is a Moslem; so, too, are at least a third of his nation. In this most populous of the newly independent African states, the entire northern tier of provinces is solidly Islamic. The grand total of Moslems in the nation may run as high as 13,000,000.

In 1948 a Moslem Congress of Nigeria was organized "to unite solidly" the country's followers of Mohammed, and "to cooperate in spreading Islam, to accelerate its progress as the religion of humanity, and to maintain close relations with related societies in Mecca, Cairo, Khartoum, and England." By 1951 the Congress leaders were ready to hold a conference in Benin City attended by fraternal delegates from Sierra Leone, Ghana, and Gambia. There it was decided to form a West African Moslem League embracing the four countries.

Islam has long been an ingrained, consolidated force in the life of northern Nigeria, but its introduction into southern Nigeria is comparatively recent. The Yoruba of western

Nigeria began to accept this faith only at the beginning of the present century, and progress at first was slow. The "missionaries" were Hausa traders from the north, considered by most Yorubas to be the worst possible element in Islam. Early converts were few, and they were ridiculed and ostracized. Gradually, however, as in Ibadan, Islam attracted prominent figures, civic leaders, and enterprising merchants. Arabic scholars also traveled down from the north to add a professional touch to the teaching and preaching of the ordinary believers who proselytized in the course of their business.

Today there are hundreds of mosques in Ibadan, and the number of Islamic schools steadily increases. A society known as The Ansar-U-Deen is particularly interested in promoting education of a Western type among Moslem children.

In Lagos, the swarming federal capital, Islamic activity is at an all-time peak. There I met Dr. Babs Fafunwa (his doctorate is from New York University), who was at that time in charge of personnel and public relations for Esso. He has since become a member of the faculty of the new University of Nigeria at Ensuka. He described himself as "a Moslem by birth and conviction, but a *liberal* Moslem." When I asked how he would define "liberal" in this context, he said: "A liberal Moslem believes in the old saying, 'A man may sleep in the mosque and beat his head to a pulp against the ground [in prayer], but if he goes out and does harm to his fellow man he is no Moslem.' "

He told me that he had just accepted the Education Chairmanship of his sect, the Islamic Society, which was organizing secondary schools at a steady rate. He was also founder and chairman of the Moslem Association of Nigeria, which was in the midst of a fund-raising campaign to launch a recreational and educational program among young people, "essentially like that of the Y.M.C.A.'s and Y.W.C.A.'s."

"There is more delinquency among our young people than we like to admit," he informed me. "We Moslems have been the 'poor relations' for a long time, especially in educational opportunities. Christian missions ran what schools there were. Our parents didn't want us to go for fear that we would be bilked into renouncing Islam. I deliberately lied about my religion, and claimed to be a Christian, in order to get into secondary school. It nearly broke my father's heart. Nigerian Moslems, especially in the north, have been reactionary about education, fearing it as a tool of infidels, and not having sense enough to do something about it themselves. Now this is changing, and it's changing fast, but we still have an awful lot of uneducated and frustrated young people roaming around the cities. We're beginning to do something about it, and we will do more."

When I asked Dr. Fafunwa if he expected Islam to become the national religion of Nigeria, he answered: "That doesn't really matter to me. What Nigeria needs is religious toleration of the broadest kind. I must say that Christians in this country are decidedly less tolerant of Moslems than the other way around."

"Of course," he added, "we have some pretty hot sectarian differences among ourselves."

These "hot sectarian differences" are symbolized by the presence in Lagos of no less than three "cathedral" mosques, and three chief Imams: one for *orthodox* Moslems, one for Ahmadis, and one for the *liberal* Islamic Society.

Ahmadiyya: a Modern Moslem Missionary Society

I have mentioned several times the weaving of Ahmadiyya influences into the emerging Islamic patterns. This is easily the most active and extensive Moslem missionary movement in tropical Africa, yet its roots are not African at all. The sect was born in the Punjab, and its missionary headquarters is in Pakistan. In the late nineteenth century, Mirza Ghulam Ahmad, the founder, claimed to be the promised Mahdi and Messiah, but he was condemned by orthodox Moslems as an imposter and heretic. After his death in 1908, there was a split in the movement between those who accepted Ahmad's claim to be "the Seal of the Prophets" and those who insisted that he was a great reformer of the faith, but no more than that. Extensions of this breach are to be found in Africa, but the main thrust of Ahmadiyya missionary work stems from the original sect.

Ahmadiyya influence reached the east and west coasts of Africa almost simultaneously in 1916. It came as a reform movement, a liberalizing influence, seeking to reconcile the teachings of Islam with modern education, and its methods were cued by the techniques and terminologies of Christian missionary efforts. The first Ahmadi teachers, natives of what is now Pakistan, made no bones of their distaste for the magic and occultism practiced by many Moslems. They called for a firming-up of slack devotions, and there were stern summonses to give women a higher place in religious life. Strikingly, there was vigorous endorsement of monogamy. The key Koranic passage quoted was: "Of women who seem good in your eyes, marry but two, or three, or four and if ye still fear ye shall not act *equitably* [italics mine], then one only." Ahmadi missionaries taught that it was nonsense to expect a man to act "equitably" to more than one wife.

In Ahmadi doctrine, Mohammed is "the best of prophets and the best of creation." Complete union with God is impossible for those who do not know him and his teachings. Among the ten conditions of membership in Ahmadiyya is a pledge by the applicant to "establish a brotherhood" with the founder, Ahmad, by obeying his discipline "in everything good."

The big break with Moslem orthodoxy is the teaching that Allah's revelation is continuous. Prophets like Ahmad can still appear in Mohammed's wake, though only "one who is a follower of his and bears his seal." Allah has spoken, however, through other messengers—Zoroaster, Buddha, Krishna, and Rama Chandra. These too were divine spokesmen, deserving honor. They guided their peoples in the paths of right.

The founder of Ahmadiyya taught a unique Christology with which, in debate, modern Ahmadis love to raise Christian hackles: Jesus was crucified all right; no doubt about that. But because of the Galilean's genuine righteousness, Allah rescued him from an ignominious end of the cross by causing him to fall into a swoon resembling death. He was in this coma when laid in the tomb, and on the third day Jesus recovered consciousness and "arose." After a secret meeting at which he assured his disciples that he was indeed alive, Jesus journeyed to Afghanistan and Kashmir, where some of the lost tribes of Israel had previously settled. It was in Kashmir that he finally and truly died. There, on Khan Yar street of Springagar, visitors may see *Isa Sahib,* the tomb of Jesus the Prophet. But the soul of Jesus is not there. Like that of all righteous men, it has gone to Allah.

The response of the usually tranquil and tolerant Christian scholar, Geoffrey Parrinder, reflects the tartness of Christian reaction to *this* particular bit of Ahmadi historical theology: "It would be extraordinary if [Ahmad] should know better than the disciples of Christ in the first century who wrote the Gospels! The tomb might be that of one of the early Nestorian Christian missionaries in India."

If Christians are stung by the aggressive tactics of the Ahmadiyya, they must still admit that it is a far more progressive and broad-minded movement than any to be found within orthodox Moslem ranks. The *ulama* (those trained in Islamic law) and *malamai* (Moslem clerics), based in northern Nigeria, are bitterly opposed to the "heresies" of the Ahmadis, fearing their divisive influence. Anti-Ahmadiyya propaganda has thus far kept the movement small in northern towns, but there are signs of its growing appeal to the *évolué* class. Impact of this kind is even more marked in the orthodox Saltpond and Colony regions of Ghana, and in Sierra Leone. In the important towns of south-western Nigeria, there is a rapid influx of Admadi strength. A piety tax (*zakat*) is levied by the Admadiyya on their followers, and since many converts are substantial merchants, there are surprisingly large funds at the disposal of the missionary effort. Some of these funds are shrewdly channeled into primary and secondary schools—a highly appealing move in a nation hungering and thirsting after the magic of learning. Even more impressive, and "heretical," schools are being established for girls as well as for boys, a startling departure from tradition.

The Ahmadiyya impulse stands apart from all prior Moslem operations in Africa in its importation of incentives and designs utterly different from those of traditional African Islam. While this was bound to arouse sectarian strife, it has also excited interest in liberal Islam among those who are impatient with the old and eager to get on with the new. A Moslem autocrat like the Emir in Kano, northern Nigeria's Islamic capital, is an unyielding conservative in a time of radicals. He is appalled enough at the heterodoxy of the prophetship of Ahmad, but even more is he coldly furious at such odious Ahmadi practices as permitting women to enter mosques to pray behind the men, and encouraging brides to be present at their weddings to give consent! The Emir is a man accustomed to the wielding of unchallenged power among the faithful. From his medieval palace in Kano's "Old City" he rules a feudal hierarchy of nobles and elders, whose titles and prerogatives, though they now include many new "winds of change" duties, are inherited from centuries past. The Ahmadiyya, with their insistence upon the right to revamp and up-date Moslem law, are a real threat to traditional authority. Their spirited social welfare and educational programs are foreign and abhorrent to the ancient temper.

Every Man a Propagator of the Faith

Interest in liberal Islam has now outstripped even the Ahmadiyya. Lagos, as indicated, has not only its Ahmadiyya Friday Mosque, but, as well, the Friday Mosque of the Jama-At-Ul Islamiyya, the Islamic Society, presided over by Chief Imam Hadji L. B. Agusto.

In the old quarter of Lagos, at 21/23 Bamgbose Street, I visited a rambling city compound fronting the street with two bare, dark offices. Behind is a closed courtyard bordered by a square of connecting stucco buildings. Countless children were playing about, and I caught sight of a couple of women swiftly disappearing behind ground-level doors. There was an outside flight of creaking wooden stairs which I climbed to reach the Imam's personal apartment. There, the tiny front room was all but choked with pieces of massive Victorian wood and velour furniture. Books, file folders, and documents were piled about in helter-skelter heaps.

Hadji L. B. Agusto, just awakened from his nap, walked in from the darkness of the rear of the apartment, dressed in a flowing blue-printed traditional *boubou.* A husky old man, very sure of himself, he is reputed to have made two fortunes—one in the drug business and another in law.

In response to my first question (What future did he see

for Islam in Africa?), he began to talk and did not stop, except occasionally to ask me rhetorically if I understood, for one hour and fifteen minutes. He described his entire history as a Moslem leader from 1910, when he began to work in the orthodox Central Mosque. In a burst of enthusiasm he had formed the Moslem Literary Society, a kind of Great Books discussion group, but after six years of discouraging experience with the moss-backed *malamai*, he decided it was impossible to bring enlightenment into the Central Mosque. "Jesus was right," he said; "You can't put new wine into old bottles."

At about this time the Ahmadiyya arrived in Lagos. Agusto greeted the movement with undisguised pleasure and became one of its earliest backers. A graduate of pharmaceutical school, he launched a drug business which was soon thriving, and with his savings he went off to London for several years of study which ended with a law degree.

Back home in Lagos he renewed his Ahmadiyya activities, but with a creeping sense of disillusionment. His own theological liberalism had advanced several notches, and the dogma of Ahmad's divine messiahship stuck in his throat. While the Ahmadiyya were doing much in the field of education, it struck Agusto that they were more interested in evangelism than in spreading a modern school system. "It seemed to me," he said, "that Ahmadi missionaries were uncomfortably like their Christian counterparts in this respect. They were more anxious to foster their particular brand of Islam than they were to foster African progress."

In time, Agusto made a clean break. With others who shared his views he organized the Jama-At-Ul Islamiyya, dedicated to "education, modern thinking, the use of reason, the higher things of life for Africa."

Then, with this animated personal history out of the way,

he shifted his tremendous girth on the divan, leaned forward meditatively, and began to speak of the broader scene:

"Islam is spreading fast in tropical Africa. I have no statistical studies to prove it. They don't exist. But all you have to do is look around. After Billy Graham had been here a while he began to talk like an alarmed man, and some of my Catholic missionary friends have been sending frantic reports back home."

He spoke of his wish that there might be some basic studies undertaken by people capable of determining statistically the "real situation" in African religion. "What is meant when it is said that Christianity is 'losing'? Does this mean that Christians are no longer able to recruit new converts from the non-Moslem populations in Africa? Does it mean that formerly pious Christians, or nominal ones, are falling away from the churches for the mosques? If Islam is 'winning,' in what parts of Africa is it gaining? Is it in areas where Islam has had a strong foothold before, or are there advances also where Christianity appeared to be firmly established? Or is it in the marginal areas, the transitional zones, between predominantly Moslem populations and non-Moslem ones, such as our Middle-Belt here in Nigeria? Is Islam moving ahead in the villages, or only in the towns and cities? How it is doing among the *évolué* class, our rising elite? And among the lower-income groups? These are some of the questions I wish we had factual answers to. Then we would know where we stood and what ought to be done."

Once again Agusto moved his great frame and drew breath. He was warming up to a flight of speculation, statistics or no:

"I'll tell you why I *think* Islam is winning. For one thing it isn't entangled in a web of missionary organization. The Ahmadiyya are organized, just like a Christian group. But the rest of us—orthodox or liberal—operate on the principle of every man a propagator of the faith. It's like our African political slogan of 'one man, one vote.' A man may be a well-off lawyer, as I am, or he may be an illiterate, penniless barterer traveling through the back country selling his goods in animist villages; but whatever else he is, he is a missionary for Islam. No matter where he goes on his journeys he pauses at the appointed time to say his prayers to Allah. People watch and listen and are impressed."

I had heard stories of how itinerant traders sparked curiosity about Islam as they walked from village to village in a bush or jungle area, but it was a mystery to me how this curiosity was consolidated into an organized Moslem community. Agusto supplied an answer: "Pack-carrying traders sometimes find a spot they like and settle down. Before you know it they have become self-appointed marabouts, clerics. A congregation begins to cluster around such a man. He offers instruction in the Koran, and marks off a square area for prayer with four logs. The congregation gradually grows, attracting the young people little by little. In time a mud mosque is built over the prayer area, and another center of Islam is established.

"That's the way it might happen in a village, but you must remember also that young men are leaving their villages these days in a flood. They hear exciting stories about city life. I believe you Americans have a song about 'How are you going to keep them down on the farm after they've seen Paree?' Well, it's that way here. Young men want to throw off the domination of elders, which is so much a part of our traditional life. And they want to make money with which to marry. So they head for the larger towns. For most of them it is a sorry experience at first. Life is lonesome and confused. They work long hours, or they roam about listlessly looking for employment. All the close contacts of the village are gone. They are far away from the spiritual security of their village cult. At night they come back to their hovels. There is no one to dance with, or pray with. Then one day someone says, 'What do you know about Islam? Come with me and take a look.' He does, and he finds himself welcomed into a community where there is praying and strong talk of how all things come from Allah, and how all men are brothers in the teachings of Mohammed. He finds, too, that there is a social side to Islam with great appeal. There are many dancings and drummings and festivals. The leaders are Africans just like himself. Often they receive no pay for their religious work, but have some other occupation with which they support themselves. In no time at all he is on his way to becoming a believer. And when he does become a believer, he never feels alone and lost again. No matter what town he tries for employment, he can look up a marabout to further his instruction, and he can find brothers with whom to eat and pray and dance.

"Some of our Christian friends are forever criticizing us because we do not demand of converts that they cut themselves off completely from their old religious roots. It is marked up against us as being 'shocking' that city Moslems, when they return to their villages, fall right back into traditional animist practices. I am afraid that this attitude reflects a rather 'shocking' lack of appreciation for the virtues of tolerance and adaptability. I know that you can quote scripture, Moslem or Christian, to 'prove' any side of an argument. But there is a saying of Mohammed's: 'In religion there is no compulsion.' What is to be gained from rushing people along faster than they are able to go? A new religious faith penetrates best when it penetrates slowly, and when it retains respect for what is of value in old ideals and practices. Now there are limits to this, of course. But our approach is very different in this respect from that of most Christian missionaries. I go to Mass every once in a while, and I often visit the services of various Protestant congregations. In general I am appalled at how few *African* characteristics they have. The only adaptability there seems to be is the compulsion on Africans to adapt to European religious forms. Now this, in my opinion, is no way to plant a spiritual movement deep in African soil. For a religion to prosper in this land it has to be Africanized.

"You may have noticed the new Catholic cathedral being built along the Marina. I marvel at how little the Bishop seems to learn from his experience. He is a fine man and a very effective organizer, but he never seems to ask himself why it is that so many Africans journey *through* Catholicism into Islam. It comes back again to this failure to understand the impossibility of a total break all at once with one's religious past. An African youth, once he gets some education, looks around for ways to prove that he is a 'new' man. Catholicism attracts him because of its cross-grained attitude toward paganism, so he becomes a convert. In a sense, he explodes out of his tradition. He and others like him gather in a community which is totally estranged from the rest of the village or tribe. But as he grows older he finds this isolation less and less appealing. Islam offers him an alternative. He need not go back to animism to recapture his African identity. He finds peace in a higher religion which is thoroughly integrated with African life.

"Our task is to make this journey from paganism to Islam as free from anxiety as possible. There's enough anxiety in African life without our adding still more. New converts are not expected to become Moslem saints over night. We encourage them to feel their way into the more rigorous duties and obligations. We ask only that they promise to be faithful in their efforts to learn more about the religion of the Prophet, and that they will educate their children in Islamic faith.

"Islam has this big advantage here. Its outlook has not been shaped by the West, as Christianity's has. The gulf between the African and European Christianity is tremendous. There's no difficulty in Islam about understanding the African mind. I have heard Christian missionaries say that Islam is a religion of desert nomads; that it cannot possibly understand the mental workings of an African farmer. Well, in many ways it is far better prepared to understand the African farmer than Western Christianity is. Some of the best farmers we have are Moslems.

"How do you suppose the celibacy of the Catholic priesthood looks to an African farmer? An African farmer cannot conceive of himself as being a full man until he gets married. The joining of male and female, fertility, the rhythms of the physical world, particularly the sexual ones, all of this has roots in the earth for Africans. Catholic priests reject it for themselves. Protestant missionaries often give the impression that they consider it to be lewd. Islam, on the other hand, appreciates the mystery of fertility. The physical charms of women and the desire that burns in men's veins do not frighten a Moslem marabout—or his wife. Western Christianity long ago turned its back on the fertility aspects of religion. African Islam makes no such mistake.

"There is much talk of Islam's loose morality. Usually this means our failure to force monogamy on our converts. It is quite true that Moslem teaching accepts polygamy. But let's ask why so many Africans feel as they do about polygamy. Is it because they are immoral? Not at all. For the African, life circles around the continuity of the family. In our traditional society there has been no place for the unmarried woman. Many Africans fear that a monogamous Africa would leave multitudes of women unmarried, and would actually encourage sexual license. The natural center of our life is the family. Polygamy is felt to be the way to keep widows and unmarried girls within, rather than outside, the securities of family life. All of the more enlightened branches of Islam in Africa are encouraging monogamy. But changes of this kind are not accomplished by fiat. The transfer from polygamy to monogamy makes increasing good sense to the city African, but the same is yet far from true in the villages.

"That reminds me of something else. There's a great deal of tongue-clucking among Christians because we do not forbid sacrificial rites among our converts. Again it is a case of long-established tribal loyalties which call for sacrifices as a contribution to the common good. Sacrifice means giving up something dear. A plain villager in following the ways of his fathers will without hesitation make an offering of an ox as his contribution to the tribal cult that nurtures him spiritually, heals his sick, and guarantees protection for his children. If he becomes a Christian, he is frowned upon for so much as offering a chicken. We fail to see how this stiff-necked, judgmental attitude really helps a man to re-think his relationship with God.

"We are not inclined, in the name of morality, to make demands which are completely out of the reach of new converts. If more Africans choose us rather than Christianity because of our greater flexibility, then I say it is to our credit rather than something we need to apologize for. This business of adaptability is a two-way street. Africans learn from Islam, but Islam also learns from Africans. There is a lot of emotion in our pattern of life. Our ancient religions are very intimate, even sentimental, in their human qualities. The old gods were not remote, transcendent beings. They were close and personal. Islam in tropical Africa is much less speculative and aggressive than it is in the Arab world. It has an earthier and more exuberant quality, learned from African life. So, in a way, Africans take Islam and season it to their own tastes.

"This, I say, is good, and I am genuinely happy to see that

Christian groups are beginning to be much less resistant to adaptation than they used to be. In fact, I can think of nothing less intelligent than a continuing warfare between Christianity and Islam for African souls. Differences we will always have, but one of our Moslem sages has put it very well. He says that Africa is like a hospital where the old are dying and the young are being born. Many different kinds of doctors and nurses are needed to give comfort, ease pain, dispense obstetrical skills, and care for the newborn. It's too much to expect that Christianity and Islam can be partners in this. But since both are needed, there is no sense in their being enemies. Africa is their meeting ground, not their battlefield."

Chief Imam Hadji L. B. Agusto must be fully credited with the prejudices he holds. He is frankly and avowedly a partisan and apologist for his faith, but he is also a wise and liberal man. I left his congested sitting room with the feeling that I had been in the presence of a spacious mind.

There is, of course, a seamier side to African Islam, or what might be called an all-too-human side. It merits consideration:

The Low End of the Crescent

It is not especially inspiring at the low end of Africa's Moslem crescent. Islam has no ordained priesthood, but it does have a clergy. Among the clerics of all religions, in all ages, there have been scoundrels and self-serving operators, and African Moslems seem to be cursed with an unusually high percentage of such, especially in the back-country areas. The majority of the clergy are very ignorant. Even with the best of intentions they are exceedingly weak stimulants to the intellectual development of Africans in their charge, and what is more disturbing is the way many of these clerics "muscle in" on traditional practices of magic and turn them to their own profit. Chief Imam Agusto described the techniques of pack-carrying barterers settling down and becoming marabouts of a converted village. The picture loses its charm when one of these informal Moslem clerics becomes a maker and seller of Islamic amulets to replace the pagan ones. Playing upon all the old superstitions, he convinces his converts that *his* amulets derive their magical power from Allah.

Indeed, he is likely to dissuade people from sacrificing to the old spirits by promising protection from them through his own Moslem magic, for which, of course, there is a price. Simple villagers are easy marks for this technique. A Moslem marabout makes magic amulets upon which there is writing. The traditional African belief in the power of the *word* gives these written charms a captivating appeal.

Some of these marabouts develop amazing versatility as magicians. Trimmingham describes their talismen as containing "verses from the Koran, names of angels and *jinn*, mysterious formulas, cabalistic tables." Only the marabout is capable of telling how and where they are to be used. Some fend off bad magic and turn it against its agent; some bring harm to enemies; others bless users with health, riches, children, or power—whatever is desired.

Another enticing product peddled at a profit by rascally clerics is the water used to wash Koranic texts from wooden slates. This water is bottled by a marabout and sold as "medicine." It may be swallowed or rubbed on the body, depending on the desired results. Some women use it to get their husbands to divorce them, which brings us to another of the less attractive aspects of African Islam.

There are strange contradictions in the traditional status of women in African life. Basically, a woman's function has been to bear children. Yet Africans are sometimes shocked to learn that American wives do not always have complete control of their own money. Down through history, African women were expected to do the heavy work, had very little social standing, and certainly exerted little political influence as a group. Yet the women of a village compound were the guardians of the family, and, for that matter, of the race.

Changes have been coming with the suddenness of the turn of a kaleidoscope. African nationalism has not overlooked the emancipation of women: "One man, one vote" means women, too—except in the areas where Moslem influence dominates. There the restrictions of Moslem custom resist the winds of change, not only in political participation, but in education as well—a process so essential to progress.

The Ahmadiyya and the Jama-At-Ul Islamiyya are actively seeking greater liberty and educational opportunity for women, but in areas such as Sudan, Zanzibar, and Northern Nigeria—wherever orthodoxy reigns—women live under the old incubus of seclusion and ignorance.

A bizarre feature of the role of women under orthodox Moslem influence is the encouragement given to prostitution in many markets and towns of Islamic West Africa. Bride-price practices work a real hardship where rigid Moslem social hierarchies are established. Men in the nonprivileged classes, too poor to pay the required marriage money, must do without wives. Prostitution flourishes in response to this situation, and only when it reaches unmanageable proportions is there likely to be a reaction from Moslem clergy, chiefs, and public officials. The most incongruous feature is that these prostitutes are, in one observer's words, "the freest, most versatile, and often best educated women in Islamic West Africa. They attend the women's prayer annex, not necessarily in order to find clients, and they will be found attending Koran schools."

The new Jerusalem sighted by Africa's modern leaders is

a place where women are *proper* partners, and not mere mating partners, cooks, toters of loads, bearers of children, or educated prostitutes. This means a fullness of participation which Islam, in many of its African manifestations, resists and undermines.

Attitudes of Africa's Uncommitted

There is an ancient Dahomey proverb: "A man does not run among thorns for nothing: Either he is chasing a snake or a snake is chasing him." Growing numbers of Africans look upon religious affiliation as a bed of thorns into which they are not, for the present, inclined to run. They are neither chasing nor being chased by sectarian "snakes." In areas where Islam dominates, Africans of this sort, by reason of birth and upbringing, are Moslems; but they are apt to be more nominal than pious. Where Islam, along with Christianity, is vying for attention and commitment, there is a tendency to look on with mild interest, but with little more.

"I know very little about Islam," said one of Tom Mboya's lieutenants in Nairobi. "It seems to be gaining, and maybe it gains because it is a better religion. Some of my friends are impressed because they say Moslems practice and live their religion not only in their rituals, but in the way they relate to their fellow-believers, in their nonracial attitudes, in their community life, and in their sense of personal dignity." He shrugged and went on. "Many people feel that Christianity has been part of the defrauding of Africa. They're skeptical of religions as a whole, but a little less so of Islam. It doesn't mean that they are *for* Islam, but because of their antagonism toward Christianity, they are not likely to resist Moslem activities in their circles. They themselves, meanwhile, tend to become more secular in their attitudes. Cultural revivalism and other interests of a political and economic nature increasingly engage their attention, minimizing their need for any religious commitment of a formal type."

What accounts for this point of view? It is prevalent only in a segment of Africa's population, but a particularly articulate segment. Toward Islam, blandness; toward Christianity, hostility.

First, there is a general but not sharply defined skepticism toward organized religion. This type of African is uneasy about the traditional religions of his people. He knows that Africa has no monopoly on superstition, but that it has, perhaps, more than its share. Yet, the "salvation after death" philosophies of the so-called higher religions strike him as being "sentimental." He feels that religion in his own culture has been retarding intellectually and materially; but when he looks to those parts of the world where material advances are most impressive—notably the West—he finds that Christianity is extolled while materialism is practiced. His conclusion is that such countries do not take their religion seriously, or, at any rate, that it has little to do with their economic and social strivings. Materialism is their way of life, and it gets results. Religion is a kind of fluff. It imparts certain personal satisfactions, but it is unimportant in the basic scheme of things.

To Africans who have thought things out in this fashion, modernization implies not only a separation from local superstitions, but a detachment from organized religion in general. This detachment expresses itself antagonistically toward Christianity, but less belligerently toward Islam.

A man who belongs in this category, a highly educated Ibibio from eastern Nigeria, expressed it to me this way: "Aside from authoritarian tendencies in Moslem religion, I find the political and social conservatism of Islamic communities incompatible with modernization. In Nigeria, the ruling classes of the Moslem North actually dug in their heels and resisted the independence movement. Their privileges were protected by the colonial administration. Their attitude toward modern education was a scandal. Now, with independence, the ruling classes in these Moslem areas are gradually introducing some measure of modernization, at least at a rate which will not disturb their social and political ascendency. But in a very large measure, Islam remains a bulwark against progress in those areas of Africa where Moslems predominate. It shelters the feudal hierarchy from the participation by the many in the political and economic life of their communities. In the Sudan, neither the elected civilian governments nor the present military regime have been able to dislodge the entrenched position of the fanatics who run the Mahdi movement. They've still got the Sudan by the throat."

If this seems hostile, we shall see in later pages that it is relatively mild compared to critical attitudes towards Christianity. The reaction of this type of African is usually tempered by what might be called:

The Charms of Islam

First of all there is Islam's happy disassociation from the racism of colonial regimes. Christian spokesmen justifiably call attention to the Koran's blessing on slavery and to the rollicking slave trade carried on by Moslem invaders and traders in the old days. The case carries surprisingly little weight, however, with African skeptics. Generally it is brushed aside as another piece of colonialist-Christian propaganda aimed at keeping Africa divided. Such Africans will argue that Islam, over all, has shown a much greater capacity than Christianity for supporting African national aspirations.

In specific racial terms, contact with Moslem missionaries has always been personal, warm and human. This is in great contrast to many of the representatives of Christianity with whom Africans have associated. In fact, it is to the credit of Islam that no racial barriers, whether of marriage or otherwise, have been set up in Africa. Believers are equals, racially speaking, and truly so, within their community. No mosque is ever set aside for this race or that or for this social class or that.

As long ago as the turn of the century, Edward Blyden, in his book *Christianity, Islam, and the Negro Race,* called attention to some of the more subtle features of Islam's racial attractiveness. He pointed out that, unlike Christianity, Islam has no God, Christ, Angels, or Virgin Mary symbolized as white. It has no statues, or images, or illustrated Bible-story books, suggesting that the heroes of divine salvation are all non-black.

With this psychological barrier absent, it has been easier for Africans to accept Islam as a truly indigenous religion. Nor did Moslem missionaries ever speak of defending "Arabic Moslem values," as so many Christian missionaries have spoken of upholding "Western Christian values."

Still another key factor has been the early selection of young Africans to be trained in Cairo and Khartoum as Moslem missionaries. Long before Christian groups were giving any significant opportunities for mission leadership to Africans, Islam was being spread by men who shared the fundamental feelings of African peoples because they were themselves of these peoples. They interacted without restraints of race or class. Quite aside from color, class feeling is a phenomenon which European Christian leaders have shared with the secular community. Class barriers exist in Islam, but in highly traditional forms familiar to Africans. There is otherwise a strong spirit of sharing in a Moslem community, which matches that of African village life. There is, too, within Islam an institutionalized way of caring for the poor similar to that of tribal life.

Last but not least, Islam has adjusted to African society and has not burdened its converts with demands originating in a "foreign" way of life. It satisfies different needs for different communities; it is capable of strengthening community links and family units. Its moral codes, archaic though they may be in some respects, are a potential bridge to modernization. It has been a truly moral force for the lower classes, enabling many to live dignified and self-respecting lives in the midst of bewildering change. It is capable of creating loyalty within a community and solidarity within a group, thus avoiding the fragmentations often found in the wake of competing Christian sects and denominations. These are values which are broadly respected in Africa, even by those who have no personal intention of becoming Moslems.

There is little doubt that Islam will continue to gain new members among the masses of Africans in teeming urban areas. There, alienation and social estrangement are bound to increase, and in Islam, many will find relief from their earthly misery. This will happen, especially, if the governments of these countries are unable to provide sustained economic growth which will assure employment to city dwellers, as individualism replaces the old securities of kinship and tribal life, and as planned industrial development lags behind the spread of social disorganization.

For the majority of Africans, Islam has a fresh appeal. In fact, this is one of Islam's great attractions to the millions who have never before come in contact with it. Knowing nothing of its history or doctrines, an African's first brush with Islam is likely to be exicting. I was told by an African graduate student studying in Boston: "Our education at home or abroad has hardly prepared us to understand Islam. Christians are too busy in Africa trying to shelter us from all sorts of ideas in order not to 'spoil' our 'childlike qualities.' I am quite often astonished at the ignorance of a great many African Christians about the world. They have an amazing capacity to commit the Bible to memory, but at that point their curiosity comes to an end. They need to know about Islam. They need to know about the world. With knowledge, they can judge for themselves."

Islam will be judged by African intellectuals on the basis of its ability to reform itself to meet modern needs, and to help in the development of "African personality." For the masses, however, it is, and will remain, a faith "on the move": a rising crescent over an agitated continent. Whatever the shape of Africa's future, Allah seems destined to play a major role.

V

Christ's Kingdom in Africa

As I look back over my experiences in Africa I would say that one of the most "Christlike" Africans I met was Kenneth David Kaunda, the thirty-eight-year-old "Black Mamba" of African nationalism in Northern Rhodesia. Yet Kaunda is no follower of Christ, at least not in any formal sense. Christian churchmanship is as little a part of his present life as the making of fine needle-point, but he grew up in the world of "the Christian Mission" where his father was right-hand man to the missionary, and his mother the leader of women converts.

What makes a man as gentle as Kaunda turn away from the lamb of Christ and take up with the tiger of African politics? Any glib answer to this question is likely to be wrong, but the question itself goes to the root of Christianity's condition in Africa. Kenneth Kaunda cannot be understood as an isolated figure. He is a man of his time and generation, a product of the forces shaping modern Africa.

It is more than a hundred years since David Livingstone came to Northern Rhodesia to "open a path for Christianity and Commerce." At the Eighth Meeting of the Christian Council of Northern Rhodesia, held in 1959, a report was adopted which read in part: "What he [Livingstone] so nobly began would seem, under the Providence of God, to have greatly prospered. In town and country the Word of God is proclaimed and European and African Christians work and witness to its eternal power and truth."

The report goes on to speak of the combination of European scientific and technological talents and African labor, which "has made possible a high standard of material life for the European and great financial rewards for the investors behind him, while releasing vast sums, which would otherwise not have been available, for the improvement of the material lot of our African citizens."

Then there occurs this crucial paragraph:

> We should be the first to acknowledge this, and to praise God for His bountiful mercy in creating the conditions in which such an outpouring of Christian witness and man's natural skills and resourcefulness have been made possible. But while we do this we are deeply conscious of the dark underside to all this appearance of Christian work and economic progress, of the perverse tides of prejudice and fear that are running fast and deep in the minds of our fellow-countrymen, of the pressures (outside as well as within our borders) of an increasingly self-confident African nationalism that is poisoning the souls of large numbers of Europeans and Africans, and of the lack of a firm and realistic relationship of mutual confidence and respect between our European and African citizens.

How does Kenneth Kaunda fit into this "dark underside" of Africa's encounter with the "Christianity and Commerce" for which Livingstone opened a path?

Near Chinsali, in the remote northeast corner of Northern Rhodesia, is Lubwa, a Mission of the Church of Scotland. In the huge, incongruous stone church at Lubwa is a tablet memorializing the evangelism of David Kaunda, first preacher of the Christian Gospel to the BaBemba of the Lubwa area. For eight years this stalwart native of Nyasaland pled his cause in lonely isolation amongst a strange tribe. His success was so great that in 1913 the Church of Scotland Mission appointed Mr. MacMinn to build at Lubwa a permanent station.

David Kaunda trekked back to Nyasaland to find a wife among his own Tonga people, and he returned with a woman who spoke fluent English and had been mission-trained in domestic science. Kenneth, the second son, was born in 1924. His mother, remembered as a kind but strict disciplinarian, and as a fervently pious woman, raised her two sons and two daughters on a regular diet of night and morning prayers. She was matron of the Girls' Boarding School and a teacher.

From his birth, Kenneth was exposed to the best of Christian missionary influence. He had the extraordinary opportunity, so seldom open to Africans of his generation, of beginning school at the age of seven, and he received the choicest kind of education then available to any African child.

Aside from an occasional visit by a District Commissioner, Kenneth saw few white faces except those of the dominie, MacMinn, and the mission doctor. Kenneth's father was left in charge of the Mission much of the time while MacMinn toured the villages to preach. When MacMinn was at Lubwa he was engrossed in his translation of the Bible into CiBemba. Not content to use the King James Version, this dedicated Scot insisted on working from original Greek and Hebrew texts, and he went to great pains to discover from the village elders just the right CiBemba words for his translation. Dr. Brown was no less conscientious. He marched tirelessly from village to village on medical rounds. His wish to be one with the people among whom he worked was so great that he left firm instructions that he be buried in the African fashion, not in a coffin but wrapped in a blanket. His grave at Lubwa lies alongside that of his old colleague David Kaunda.

Life at Lubwa was a vibrant affair compared to the normally listless ways of the BaBemba. A thriving brick and tile enterprise supplied materials for an expanding number of structures: a church, school, missionaries' housing, and a hospital. Women came out from Scotland to nurse and to teach, but not one was allowed to stay who would not or could not learn CiBemba.

The whites lived up on "missionary hill" while Kenneth's family lived in a house close to the school, but there was no segregation either in work or worship, and there was much family socializing back and forth.

MacMinn's position as "master" was clear. He was accepted by the villagers as headman of their community, and, in the best African tradition, he was "available" to his people.

Mrs. Kaunda guided her children toward a life of serving the church. The two boys and one of the girls became teachers; the other daughter took up nursing in the hospital.

All of this is worth noting because the situation was not unique. The admirable qualities of the Lubwa Mission can be duplicated in many parts of Africa. There are other sides to the Christian mission picture, as we shall see, but there are also the Lubwas. Still a Kenneth Kaunda no longer cares for the Church in which he was nurtured; and he cannot be written off as just an ingrate or a riddle.

When Kaunda toured the United States in the spring of 1960, he was to have been our house guest in Boston. Snags in his traveling schedule cut Boston out of his itinerary. For me, a visit to Northern Rhodesia some months later was an opportunity at last to meet Kaunda. His leadership of the United National Independence Party clearly marks him for future eminence in African affairs. Northern Rhodesia has not yet become part of the "new" Africa. Its overwhelming African majority is dominated by a relative handful of white settlers, administrators, and commercial and mining men. But if Kaunda survives the restless days ahead, he is likely to become Northern Rhodesia's first black prime minister, for his place in the pantheon of modern African folk heroes is already high. He is the "lion of Rhodesia," Central Africa's man of destiny.

Lusaka, Northern Rhodesia's pastel capital, has a posh hotel, the Ridgeway, built to house guests of the great mining companies, official visitors, commercial travelers, and junketing Europeans and Americans. It was there that I first met Kaunda, but only after a train of events that has its own bearing on Christianity's current position in Africa.

My arrival at the Ridgeway coincided with a full-scale race-relations conference called by the United Northern Rhodesia Association. It was a unique meeting for Central Africa, bringing together leading white officials, industrialists, and mining magnates with noted black educators, intellectuals, and nationalist spokesmen. Kaunda was not present. He was due back in Lusaka in a day or two from a political tour of upcountry areas.

About one hundred delegates spent the afternoon listening to carefully prepared papers on worsening relations between the races.

I sat at dinner with a small group which included a white statesman of the Federation of Rhodesia and Nyasaland. To save him embarrassment he will be nameless. He drank too much, and the more he drank the more garrulous and abusive he became. He had spoken at first of "blacks." Soon they became "kaffirs," an apartheider's equivalent for "niggers." He was sick and tired of "the bloody agitation of that damned kaffir, Kaunda," but even more he was nauseated by United States' policy toward African nationalism. "I hate America's guts," he bellowed at me in a particularly fierce outburst of drunken rage. This was followed immediately by reassurances that he meant nothing personal—and wouldn't I have a drink? It was a saddening performance by one of Rhodesia's top white personalities, a man of substance, and a prominent lay member of his Christian denomination.

Also at the table was the director of African personnel for one of the large copper mining companies, a Scot. The more the inebriated statesman raved, the more the Scot squirmed. Later, in the lounge, he spoke to me most earnestly. He told me of his twenty-two years of experience in Northern Rhodesia, dealing with "the natives." "As a religious man I have prayed each night these twenty-two years that I might do right by the native. After twenty-two years I think I can honestly say that I know the African and what he's like."

At a conference buffet luncheon the next day, I spotted a young African, tray in hand, who seemed to be without a companion. We sat down together and fell immediately into conversation about his work. He was attending the conference in his capacity as assistant editor of a journal published by the mining company of which the Scot was personnel director. He was a sober, intelligent young man, who spoke easily of his work.

The personnel chief saw me talking with his African employee and hurried over. With inner horror I watched that young man's personality transform itself before my eyes. From the soft-spoken, confident professional, who had been telling me about editorial operations on a mine journal, he turned in a flash into a grinning, subservient, *bwana*-salaaming semi-idiot. This was the African our praying, twenty-two-year settler "knew"!

The statesman and the personnel director have more to do than they could possibly understand with the indifference of a Kenneth Kaunda toward the Christian church. The Christian mission of Kaunda's youth, like most of its counterparts, suffered from an understandable vice. It could not bring itself to introduce its pupils to the skeleton in its own closet: the spiritual indifference of the civilization it represented; the fact that Christian idealism was the hostage of other gods in the everyday world of Western commerce and statecraft. The MacMinns, the Dr. Browns, and the Lubwas of Africa could be equated with Western civilization only within the walls of the mission compound. Beyond those walls was confusion and disillusion. Before he actually experienced it, how could a Kenneth Kaunda, or the thousands of others who owed their first knowledge of the Western World to the mission schools, know that the white priests and pastors from Europe and America had long since lost the leadership of their own people?

After the buffet luncheon, I drove out of Lusaka to the far reaches of dusty, wind-swept Matero suburb, a sprawling web of ugly, boxlike stucco huts which house the African population of the capital city. The residential areas of the city itself are for whites only. Baking in the sun, at the end of a gravel road that trails off into the bush, stands the headquarters of the United National Independence Party—a hovel with a rusty corrugated roof. Several children were playing in front, and as I walked from the car they set up a chant of "*kwacha, kwacha*" (freedom) to let me know, I guess, that they were Kaunda supporters. Holding down this bastion of power, which strikes such terror into the hearts of so many of Northern Rhodesia's whites, was Sikota Wina, one of Kaunda's chief lieutenants. Wina is a tall, heavy-lidded young man with a reputation for deeply rooted anti-white feelings. A boy of about seventeen was waiting with two letters in his hand, and Wina fished through his pockets for enough money to give the boy so that he could post the letters. I noticed that there was no telephone. The office furnishings consisted of two ancient desks, several battered chairs, and a small mimeograph machine.

Wina told me that Kaunda had not yet returned from the north, but that he was expected back at any time. I told him I would be at the Ridgeway. Then we talked for a while about Wina's younger brother, who is studying in the United States. I left to a recessional chorus of more "*kwachas*" from the children.

The next day, at 5 P.M., a bellboy knocked at my hotel door. Two gentlemen were waiting in the lobby to see me. They were Wina and Kaunda.

Kenneth Kaunda is a handsome, beautifully proportioned African. His complexion is very dark; his eyes are deep brown. He has a magnificent smile, and a gentle, almost shy, manner.

His greeting was affectionate. He apologized for his appearance, for his brown leather jacket was still covered with dust of the road. He had just returned by jeep from his tour and had come to see me before returning home to clean up.

We went into the lounge, where Kaunda ordered milk. Wina and I asked for coffee. Kaunda is a puritanical self-disciplinarian. He is a nonsmoker, a nondrinker, and a vegetarian. There is a touch of gray in his black hair, which he combs upright in Swahili fashion.

He told me of his long hard journey through the areas bordering on the Congo. The people, he said, were greatly stirred by Congo freedom. "They have made up many sayings about freedom on the other side of the river: 'half the river free, the other half not'; 'the fish on one side free, the fish on the other side not.' They say that Welensky's troops were sent to the border to shoot at freedom as it came across the river."

As he sipped his cold milk, he spoke of the crowds that had greeted him. "Over and over again," he said, "there would be gatherings of twenty thousand or more. Sometimes they had been waiting several days for my arrival. There were washouts. The jeep kept breaking down. I couldn't hold to a schedule; but once the people had gathered from the surrounding villages, they would just wait. And for the *first* time, I had some help from missionaries; from all kinds of missionaries—Catholics, Anglicans, Church of Scotland. They provided me with public address systems in some places, and helped organize food facilities where the crowds had gathered.

"Everywhere I pled with the people to remain calm and non-violent in thought, word, and deed, to make no foolish moves."

"Do you worry about the extent of your authority over your people?" I asked. "Do you worry about whether you can keep them non-violent?"

"Yes, I worry," he answered, and suddenly he looked very tired.

When Kenneth Kaunda was twenty-two, he held the highest educational qualifications then available to an African in Northern Rhodesia. He had in his hand a teaching certificate and a successful pass of Standard VIII at the Munali Secondary School. He returned to Lubwa to teach at the Boys' Boarding School, where he became at once the missionary's right-hand man, just as his father had been. Soon he was made headmaster of the school, and he might have spent the rest of his life this way. Instead he stayed only a year. Kaunda had decided that it was time for him to have some wider experiences in the world.

Heading for the Copperbelt, he found work as a Welfare Assistant at the Nchanga Mine. Nineteen hundred and forty-seven, he says, was the most crucial year of his life. For the first time, he bruised himself against the color bar, and it was a shocking experience. He found himself in the midst of Europeans who treated him not as a fellow human being, but as a "munt" and "kaffir."

In 1946, Dauti Yamba had formed the African Welfare Association, which was later to become the parent of the African National Congress. Kaunda became a member of the Welfare Association's Nchanga local, and he had another first experience: He heard people of his own race seriously discussing politics.

A few months at Nchanga was enough. Kaunda went back to teaching and was named headmaster of the Mufulira School. When the African National Congress was formed in 1948, he was one of the first to join. Soon, political activity was consuming all of his time. Again he resigned from teaching, packed up, and went back home. He wanted to set up some kind of business and build for himself a political base.

Welcomed by his mother to the old Lubwa home, he became a trader in secondhand clothes, which were then available at very low cost in the Belgian Congo. He would pedal his bicycle through 300 miles of bush to the Congo border, buy bales of old clothes, consign them to a trucking company, and then wheel back to Lubwa in time to unload his stock when the truck arrived. The leg muscles and lung capacity built up by this astonishing enterprise sustained him when he later cycled all over the Northern Province while organizing branches of the African National Congress. His feats on a bicycle are part of his "charisma" as a leader.

Kaunda's disenchantment with Christianity was by this time well under way. He clashed sharply with his old missionary friends at Lubwa over Welensky's proposals to federate Southern Rhodesia, Northern Rhodesia, and Nyasaland. In an open letter to the missionary in charge he quoted from Shaw's *Man of Destiny:*

"When the Englishman wants a new market for his adulterated Manchester goods he sends a missionary to teach the Natives the

Gospel of Peace. The Natives kill the missionary, he flies to arms in defence of Christianity, fights for it, and takes the market as a reward from heaven."

If you intend being of service to the British Government in the way described by Shaw, you have come at the wrong time. Our forefathers killed no Europeans in this Protectorate, and we are going to make sure we kill no European, missionary or otherwise for political reasons—Nay we won't—Reverend sir. Preach how you may we shall struggle for our nation's survival within the British Scope of struggling. We are not struggling against the British Government, but against the Federal case.

By 1953, Kaunda was recognized as the organizing wizard of the African National Congress. As General Secretary he called for a boycott of meat markets because African women were required to line up outside at a hole in the wall, while whites were served inside at the counter. When police arrested some of the women taking part in this protest against the color bar, Kaunda swore he would never eat meat again. He hasn't.

The years since 1953 have included a prison term (for possessing publications the Government had declared to be prohibited reading—among them several books on Gandhi's campaigns of non-violence), a visit to the United Kingdom to attend a Labour Party Commonwealth Conference, a mysterious chest ailment, and trips to Tanganyika, India, and Ghana, where many months were spent on a study of non-violent techniques of revolutionary action.

The story of Kaunda's break with the African National Congress, and his formation first of the Zambia Congress and then of the United National Independence Party, is better told by others than by me. Kenneth Kaunda as a symbol of Christianity's plight in Africa is an established phenomenon. It is the plight of seeing many of the Church's most talented products, men and women, who at first gave themselves in full confidence to the proclaimers of the Gospel, suffer the great disillusionment. And the basis of this disillusionment is that the Church, in the complexity of a changing society, does not possess the power to counterbalance forces in the secular world. Added to this is a conviction that the Western part of the Church is inclined to practically unlimited adjustment to the ideologies and interests of Western society.

Beachheads in a Restless Land

Amid all the disillusion, backsliding, and actual hostility, a crucial fact still stands out: In the whole of tropical Africa one in ten of the population professes to be a Christian. Those who predict the death of African Christianity in the turbulence of achieving and consolidating independence may have too quickly dismissed the conscience and creativeness of a powerful faith. Africa's situation is one of tremendous challenge to the Church, and John Vernon Taylor, in his book *Christianity and Politics in Africa,* describes it this way: "At a time when men are moving into deep tides of emotion, grappling with complicated problems in the midst of rising tensions, and laying out the foundations of future nations, the Church is more than ever needed to proclaim the Word which God is speaking, to demonstrate the way of Christ, and to offer her own embracing fellowship for the healing of nations."

I spoke earlier of the late Bishop Dagadu, Ghana's great-hearted Methodist leader. Just before I left Accra he came to my room at the Ambassador to say good-by. He wanted to know what impressions I had gained in Ghana of religious sentiments. From his point of view I had a discouraging picture to paint. It was difficult, I told him, to find Ghanaian leaders in politics, in the professions, or in the arts who are enthusiastic churchmen. Dagadu, a man of tremendous girth, slumped in his chair as I recounted some of my interviews. His brown eyes filled with tears, and he asked if I would join him in a word of prayer. I did. Afterwards he drew a deep breath, wiped a handkerchief over his moist face, and began to talk. It was almost as if he were speaking to himself and to the world. There was an exalted, impersonal quality in his voice. It was a soliloquy on how he had spent his life, and what he had spent it for. He was at that moment the embodied voice of African Christianity:

"I remember when Dr. Nkrumah was jailed by the British authorities. The people used to sing:

Kwame Nkrumah's body lies amould'ring in the jail
But his soul goes marching out.

"Goes marching out of what? Out of Christianity? Ghana cannot march away from Christianity without marching away from herself. It was the Church that assumed the responsibility for educating us when no other organized force cared to do so. It was the Church in Ghana that nurtured generations of our men and women, boys and girls, spiritually, in reading and writing, in morals and manners, agriculture, organization, and administration. It was the Church in Ghana that raised up all these men who are now our statesmen and teachers and lawyers.

"And I don't mean any particular church. All of them—Methodist, Catholic, Anglican, Presbyterian, Baptist, the Salvation Army—all of them contributed; schools, hospitals, nurses' training, places of worship, centers of a pastoral ministry to the sick, the weary, the needy, and the blind! All of this Christianity brought to Ghana. But it brought something even more precious. It brought a teaching of love and obedience to God and love and respect for man. It brought Christ to make God real in our lives.

"And now these Prometheans—these leaders of ours—who

owe practically everything they are to the churches that educated them, where do they think they got their ideas of freedom and equality and social advancement? Who brought these ideas into Ghana? Who helped to blot out tribal wars and slave raids? Who gave us a common faith capable of uniting dozens of tribes, dozens of languages, and hundreds of gods into one nation?

"Everything we now call progress in Africa is a direct or indirect fruit of Christianity. It is Christianity that set the whole of Africa on fire. It is Christianity that offered us new standards of life, new values, a new sense of respect for our color and race.

"All this talk about the Church and colonialism. It sickens me. Am I a colonial? Does someone in London or New York tell me how to conduct my affairs as a Methodist bishop? I am a Ghanaian, an African. And the Methodist Church in Ghana is an African church. We are as self-administered and self-supported as Kwame Nkrumah's government.

"What is the matter with these men who revile the Church? Can't they see that everything they condemn the Church for could also be charged against the state. We all passed through the mission stage at one point or another. The missionaries came to convert us to a Christian way of life. Many of us *were* converted, and in the process we discovered something for ourselves: We discovered freedom and justice. We discovered how to organize our lives and how to run our own affairs in modern ways. We discovered how to create our own world.

"It's true that many missionaries lacked understanding of African peoples, but we no longer have mission churches in Ghana. We have African churches! African culture has a message for Christianity, just as Christianity has a message for Africa. All my life I have struggled to bring together these two messages. And now, just when the time is ripe, many of those who could do the most to help are least inclined to do so. It is a tragic situation, but Christianity itself is based on the tragedy of Christ's crucifixion. He conquered, and so will the African Church."

Dagadu rose, clasped my right hand in both of his, and said: "We need your prayers." As he left the room, I realized that I was trembling from the intensity with which he had spoken. A few months later he was dead. He stood for something large in Ghana's life. It is not dead.

Nor can one think of Christianity as fading from the African scene when it is observed in action at the Mindolo Ecumenical Center. I needed the visit to Mindolo, for only a few days before I had found myself in the midst of bloody rioting in Salisbury:

Without warning, white Rhodesian police had swooped into African homes, just before dawn, and arrested the top executives of the only all-African political party in Southern Rhodesia. The policies of the National Democratic Party, up until that point, had been firmly "nationalist" but notably restrained. The leaders had requested a meeting with the Prime Minister, Sir Edgar Whitehead, to discuss native grievances. Their answer was arrest.

The reaction in the segregated African residential townships was immediate, powerful, and historic. For the first time in Southern Rhodesia, Africans demonstrated in an organized manner. They did so, however, in a disciplined, inspired, and completely non-violent way. I was there, one of five whites to witness and marvel at the orderliness of the Highfields mass rally and protest march.

The Government's response to Highfields was to call out troops, tanks, riot squads, and all available reserve police. The Cabinet issued a series of harsh bans on all native meetings and processions. From that moment the situation steadily deteriorated.

Overnight the African townships of Highfields and Harare became scenes of riot and bloodshed. I dodged my way through the stones, tear gas, and wild scuffling at Harare, and I was horrified at the spirit of sheer ugliness which had developed on both sides. Before it ended, uniformed whites had shot at, wounded, and killed Africans for the first time in Southern Rhodesia's modern history.

Salisbury is an elegant, modern white man's city served by elegant Christian churches. I telephoned the Congregational minister, the Rev. E. E. Thrussell, to ask what Christian leaders were doing about the riots. He told me that he was meeting with several of his colleagues the next morning to discuss the situation, and I asked if I might attend. He said he would consult the others and be around to pick me up at 8:30 A.M. the following day.

He arrived looking troubled and explained that there had been objection to an "outsider" attending the meeting. I assured him that I understood, but that I would appreciate a few minutes with him. We sat down over coffee.

He said that he expected his Methodist, Presbyterian, and Anglican colleagues at the meeting. When I asked what might come out of the meeting, he said, "We are all 'moderates' and not particularly political in our approach. But we are concerned. Whether we can agree on a statement to the government, I don't know. I don't like these emergency regulations; they're foolish. The government talks about racial partnership, but it permits no initiative from the native side in working out the partnership. That's what this trouble is all about. The National Democratic Party was beginning to take some initiative, so the government retaliated. Only this time the natives didn't take it lying down."

I asked him why the Protestant clergy was meeting. "Some

of the N.D.P. people have been in touch with us. They want us to do something. Most of them, you know, are Christians," he told me.

I remembered well the older woman who had spoken to the crowd at the Highfields mass meeting. She had cried out: "The Europeans are afraid we will drive them out if we have our way. We are not anti-European. We want the Europeans to live among us, but as equals not as angels. We are Christians, not because Europeans have taught us their Christianity, but because we have Christianity in our hearts."

Thrussell went on: "It's terrible to be expected to do something, and *want* to do something, as I do. But we're in a tight spot with our congregations. Has anyone told you about Whitfield Foy? He was the Methodist minister here, and a very straightforward type on the race issue. A number of the African leaders from Harare and Highfields started coming into town on Sunday mornings to hear Foy preach. All of a sudden Foy was transferred out of Salisbury. His leading parishioners wouldn't stand for it. An occasional African in church now and then is all right. But when it began to look as if Foy was going to have an interracial church—bang!—out he went. That's the spot we're all in."

This is what I meant about needing my visit to Mindolo. The awful weakness of the Church in Salisbury was as depressing to me as the plight of its counterpart in Little Rock. But Mindolo is something else again. Situated in the heart of Northern Rhodesia's Copperbelt, it is a parklike area of a hundred bush and forest acres on the fringes of Kitwe, the largest of the copper mining towns. Near-by are five important government institutions. The Copperbelt has drawn to itself a concentration of more than 30,000 whites and 300,000 Africans. The Africans come from Uganda, Angola, Mozambique, the Congo, Tanganyika, Nyasaland, Southern Rhodesia, and South Africa. About seventy tribes are represented.

The Mindolo Ecumenical Center is an outgrowth of the old Mindolo Mission, headquarters for United Missions to the Copperbelt. By 1955 it was apparent that the Mindolo Mission was getting nowhere, and its operations were terminated. A new body, the Copperbelt Christian Service Council, was organized to brood over Mindolo's possible future; and, although it took three years to get a report out of this Council, it was worth waiting for. An entirely new and "experimental" approach was recommended, with an Independent Foundation as the base. The World Council of Churches adopted the project and listed Mindolo as an enterprise worthy of support from churches throughout the world.

The man behind the idea was the Rev. Peter Mathews, a peppery Australian Congregationalist, who became convinced that Africa's most pressing "Christian" needs were for leadership training, research and lay consultation, and conference.

With incredible energy, Mathews raised enough money from churches, trust funds, and mining companies to launch a building program and to build a staff. The Center quickly became a center of activities rarely associated in the past with missions. For example, while I was at Mindolo nineteen African writers and journalists from various parts of the continent were engaged in a stiff six-weeks' writing seminar. They were at it from 8 A.M. to 10 P.M., with time in between for rest, recreation, and devotions—but no nonsense.

Another seminar, underway at the same time, was for housewives from the Kitwe area, white and Negro, to consider the special problems presented by life in a multiracial community.

A racially mixed group of young people were on hand for a work camp. They were digging drainage ditches, laying brick for a new dormitory, and attending classes on youth leadership.

Due to arrive the next week were a dozen African labor leaders for an institute on trade union problems.

Mathews explains the Mindolo philosophy this way: "What is true of Church life on the Copperbelt is also true of the Church in most countries of the world. The Church's function has tended to shrink to the narrow circle of worship on Sundays and 'through the week' interest groups with little effective outreach into the community. The Church no longer exercises its full responsibility in many decisive areas of man's life. The purpose of Mindolo is to find new ways of making Christianity applicable to what counts in the life of Africa."

During my stay at Mindolo I read the report of a five-day conference held there on "Man and Community on the Copperbelt." The roster of participants was studded with the names of key figures in Northern Rhodesia, white and black; and the report was the most comprehensive survey of African racial, religious, social, political and economic problems I had seen in one binding.

Hindrances to the Christian witness in Africa are powerful, but the Mindolo Ecumenical Center is a potent counterforce. Racial partnership is genuine at Mindolo, and the program there is relevant to Africa's current needs. As Mathews puts it: "The Center will not become an institution of fixed pattern. Its program will change as completely as new challenges to the Christian church are understood and accepted."

Another beacon of Christian hope in Africa is the Catholic Church's impressive African cardinal, Laurian Rugambwa. This tall, modest man is an effective reminder that there is much to be said for the Catholic policy in Africa of insisting that the indigenous clergy must have qualifications comparable to their European colleagues. Because of limited educational opportunities, this has meant that the African Catholic priesthood has grown slowly, but those entering it are highly trained. The policy, too, exposes Catholicism to the charge of remaining foreign-dominated, but it has produced a Rugambwa, who is probably the shrewdest and hardest driving African church administrator on the continent.

Until he was eight, Rugambwa was a barefoot animist in Tanganyika's banana groves. He was baptized that year because his father, a tribal elder, had been converted to Catholicism. Then later, soon after he entered a White Fathers' school, he made the decision to dedicate himself to God and the Catholic Church. In 1945 he was ordained to the priesthood, and eight years later he was consecrated a bishop. His cathedral church is said to be a bat-infested structure of eucalyptus poles and handmade brick, with a corrugated iron roof, and he makes the rounds of his diocese in a battered, vintage Chevy.

His most celebrated communicant is Tanganyika's Number One Citizen, Julius K. Nyerere, the 5-foot-6½-inch, 125-pound hero of independence. Nyerere, one of twenty-six children of a polygamous Zanaki chief, went to mission school, was converted to Catholicism, and remains loyal to the faith.

Rugambwa describes Christianity as "the most precious thing that Africa has received from the West." He cites the Catholic Church as an example of fantastic progress in Africa, and he emphasizes the role of the Church as the teacher of a strong faith in God, the liberator from superstition, the proclaimer of basic human rights for the individual, the prophet of physical, social, and economic welfare, and the educator for vast numbers.

"If Christian principles inspire the Western nations in their present and future relations with Africa," he says, "all will be well. Everyone knows that Africa is in need of monetary aid and technical assistance. However, this help must be offered in a spirit of brotherly love and understanding, in a spirit of cooperation and not of domination. Recognition of his basic dignity and of the values in his own culture and tradition is what the African expects most from the Western powers."

Those who claim that Rugambwa is a "sop" offered to Africans to deter Communist advances, must be prepared to reckon with this black cardinal's alert and sophisticated talents. Far from being a mere "showpiece," he is a determined builder of Catholic Christian strength. Beginning with a powerful beachhead of 18,000,000 at least nominal Catholics south of the Sahara, he is a resolved propagator of the faith that claims his own unswerving allegiance.

Christianity's most exposed and vulnerable flank is the Republic of South Africa, where the brutal policy of *apartheid* has been carried out by white Christians in the name of Christianity. That determined breed of long-time white settlers, the Afrikaners, have traditionally seen themselves as re-enacting the Biblical role of the chosen people in a promised land, where God has ordained the black man to be a hewer of wood and a drawer of water for the white. In jest, the Dutch Reformed Church has been known as the Afrikaner Nationalist Party at prayer, but in grim reality, it has perfumed segregation and racial prejudice with scriptural self-righteousness ("If God wished the races to be equal, he would have said so in the Bible").

Dr. Hendrik Frensch Verwoerd, an agnostic in his academic and journalistic days, became an ardent churchgoer when elected to head the Afrikaner government, and he now claims that his narrow escape from assassination by an emotionally ill planter was a divine miracle in behalf of *apartheid.*

Membership in the World Council of Churches has drawn Dutch Reformed Church leaders into consultations on South

Africa's racial problems. When ten delegates from each of South Africa's eight Protestant Churches sat down with six representatives of the World Council of Churches, the conference produced a resolution highly critical of *apartheid:* "Part of the dignity of the adult man," it stated, "is the right to own land and to participate in the government; scripture provides no basis for prohibiting the mingling of the races including mixed marriage," and there is a tragic lack of "consultation and communication" between the races.

"It is our conviction that there can be no objection in principle to the direct representation of colored people in Parliament. . . . No one who believes in Jesus Christ may be excluded from any church on the grounds of his color or race. The spiritual unity among all men who are in Christ must find visible expression in acts of common worship and witness, and in fellowship and consultation on matters of common concern."

Voting records on this resolution were not made public, but at least some of the representatives of the three Dutch Reformed Churches joined Anglicans, Methodists, Congregationalists, and delegates of the two Presbyterian bodies in voicing approval.

When a storm began to blow up among the laity and some of the clergy, the Dutch Reformed Churches felt compelled to "clarify" their position. The 200,000-member Nederduitsch Hervormde Kerk, smallest of the three, repudiated the resolution and declared its approval of complete segregation. The Nederduits Gereformeerde Kerks of Cape Colony and the Transvaal, with combined memberships of over 1,200,000, reverted to their old position that "a policy of differentiation can be defended from the Christian point of view," but they insisted that black Africans, who are established residents and workers in white areas, should be granted a proper share in government.

Novelist Alan Paton, who had attended the conference as an Anglican delegate, called the statement a "most remarkable" departure from previous positions, and lauded the Dutch Reformed for their "courage."

It tells volumes about the social and political climate of South Africa that Paton could find evidence of valor in a powerful church-body's call for slightly relaxed *apartheid* within a framework of continued "differentiation." But that the statement could be made at all by the strongest spiritual voice of Afrikanerdom is something of a wonder. Verwoerd was reported to be shaken and furious. The Afrikaner Nationalist newspaper he once edited, *Die Transvaaler*, ran a sarcastic editorial, saying: "No matter how beautiful were the thoughts expressed by the consultation, their application would lead to the collapse of Christianity in South Africa."

But at least some Dutch Reformed leaders are becoming convinced that just the reverse is true. They have deeply resented the past strictures of Cape Town's Anglican Archbishop Joost de Blank, a fighting enemy of *apartheid;* and when de Blank called for ousting the Dutch Reformed Churches from the World Council if they did not mend their racial ways, the reaction in Dutch Reformed higher circles was choleric. But this was more a matter of pride than of conscience.

As the World Council conference drew to a close, Archbishop de Blank asked for the floor and begged forgiveness from the Dutch Reformed Churchmen for any hurt he might have previously inflicted upon them in his passionate campaign against *apartheid,* and in a flush of renewed cordiality, forgiveness was warmly given. Again it was Alan Paton who found hope in the exchange: "The archbishop's action, and the response to it, shows something of the new atmosphere."

If the Anglican and Dutch Reformed Churches do find themselves drawn together in mutual concern over *apartheid,* the Christian witness in South Africa will be immeasurably strengthened.

No man dramatizes the political dilemma of Christianity in South Africa more sharply than does Nobel Peace Prize winner Chief Albert John Luthuli, leader of his country's African National Congress since 1952. Luthuli, now sixty-three years old, is a convinced, practicing Christian. His integrity is unchallengeable. He has been the personification of a Christian, non-violent, reconciling resistance to *apartheid*, and there is no shadow of anti-white sentiment in him. Yet he has been regarded by the whites as the most dangerous enemy of their supremacy. He was the central figure in the Treason Trial arrests and was barred from political activity. Five days after Sharpeville, he burned his own passbook—the most hated symbol of *apartheid*. Three days later he was again jailed.

For years Luthuli has been warning that if the whites did not parley with him, a Christian and a moderate, his following would begin to melt away and African leadership would fall into harder, more aggressive hands. Luthuli's predictions are coming true. His great natural leadership is slipping away, and his Christian commitment appears to have done little for African aspirations in South Africa.

We may be certain that Luthuli was in Joost de Blank's mind when the Archbishop declared that the Church in South Africa was "at the crossroads" and that unless it could find ways of satisfying legitimate African aspirations, "it is condemning itself to extermination—and the whole of South Africa will be wide open to secularism and non-Christian creeds."

Christianity's African beachheads are powerful and impressive, and it would be nonsense to write the Church off as the loser in the great competition for African souls as long as there are Dagadus, Mindolos, Rugambwas, Nyereres, De Blanks, Patons and Luthulis. But, by the same token, it would be foolhardy not to recognize that the *majority* of Christians of all races in Africa seem tragically unprepared for their tasks.

Rebel Churches in a Restless Land

Bengt Sundkler wrote the classic study of separatist African churches. Called *Bantu Prophets in South Africa*, it lists more than eight hundred African-led "rebel" churches officially recorded by the South African government in 1945, and it adds one hundred and twenty-three more known to exist eighteen months later. Sundkler confined himself to one country, but similar studies have been, or are being, made all over Africa. Untold hundreds of thousands of Africa's statistical Christians are participating not in mission-established denominations, but in independent, come-outer churches bearing such names as the Watchmen, the Sacred Heart of Jesus Lumpa Church, the Bantu National Church, the Cherubim and Seraphim Churches, and hundreds upon hundreds more.

While Africa is not unique in this respect—similar sects have multiplied in such places as Communist China and Indonesia—the proliferation of independent churches in Africa has a special flair. Recently, for example, on the tiny, scrubby island of Likoma in Lake Nyasa, one of Nyasaland's separatist "messiahs" announced that he intended to set up headquarters. The island's most imposing structure is a huge, ugly Anglican cathedral built a century ago by native converts. It has long been a center of Anglican missionary work and a showpiece of transplanted Christianity.

The missionary priests, already harried by defections, decided upon a dramatic gesture. They divided the nave of the cathedral down the center with a row of benches, then challenged all who dared deny the church to remain on the far side of the barrier. For a long time *no one* moved. Finally, a few of the congregation's oldest members walked to the other side, and slowly others followed. But it was discouragingly clear to the priests that the separatist "prophet" had already established himself in Likoma.

Any attempt, no matter how brief, to interpret the independent churches of Africa must revolve around the inevitable tension between the white Christian West and the black African inhabitants it set out to evangelize, exploit, and rule.

The native, separatist church is *one* of the ways in which Africans respond to their encounter with Christian-Western culture. Missionaries brought to Africa not only the pristine substance of a Gospel, but the techniques and values of an entire civilization. In African eyes, certainly, the missionary thrust of the nineteenth century was the "spiritual" portion of a general European invasion of Africa. This was the way Africans first viewed it, and, to a substantial degree, the way in which they still view it. To the African, the French Catholic White Father was first of all a Frenchman; the Anglican priest was primarily an Englishman; and both wore white faces, possessed the same strange power over the written word, practiced the same medicine, and carried the same weapons. The missionary, whatever his denomination, represented to the African a civilization immeasurably stronger than his own; a civilization which, on the one hand, might overwhelm him, but which, on the other hand, might share its power with him if a prudent alliance could be made.

To put it another way, no matter how firmly and sincerely the missionary believed his aims to be different from those of the explorer, the settler, the commercial agent, and the civil servant-administrator, the African saw them *all* as being identified with a common enterprise. Nor was the African particularly off base in his evaluation. F. B. Welbourn, in his study of separatist churches in Uganda and Kenya, confirms the legitimacy of the African view:

> Although . . . missionaries differ from other Europeans in their primary emphasis on total commitment to Christ, at least the early ones were whole-hearted in their presentation of western culture in what they believed was its best form. It is only more recent missionaries, who have been affected by anthropology and, perhaps more radically, by doubts about the value and permanence of western civilization, who begin to see the difference between what is "essentially" Christian and what is "merely" western; and even they do not know where to draw the line.

What must be kept in mind, then, is that many Africans were incapable of responding to the missionary effort as a purely religious message. In a thoroughly understandable manner, they reacted *out* of their total culture *to* a total culture, and not merely to an isolated portion of it labeled "Christian."

But if missionaries offer a complete, rather than a uniquely pious, cultural package, they also behave like their countrymen of other professions and interests in withholding parts of it.

The missions brought education, and Africans responded enthusiastically; but many missionaries shared the views of settlers and colonial officials that Africans should be educated only to that point where they could take their "proper place" in the scheme of things. The "proper place," obviously, was not an equal place. Nor was there any attempt on the part of missionaries to counsel with Africans on developing a type of education which took African outlooks and philosophies into account. It was inevitable that some Africans would see not only generosity in mission education, but a form of enslavement as well.

Missionaries, in general, shared the Western belief in national self-determination and universal adult suffrage. Protestants, in particular, professed the ideal of African churches growing toward full partnership with European and American churches. If Africans were slow at first to desire ecclesiastical independence and equality, they were apt in time to want to move *very* rapidly—much more rapidly than many of the missionaries were prepared to accept. Missionary resistance at this point made it quite certain that some Africans would demand autonomy with even greater zeal.

Missionaries, no matter what their intentions, had to be supermen to overcome their built-in conviction that they represented a superior civilization. The reverse side of this coin, of course, was disrespect, even though subtle and unconscious, for all things African—and missionary attitudes were frequently anything but subtle and unconscious. Some Africans quickly saw the rationalization, humbug, and hypocrisy in this. Missionaries talked of "blessing" Africa with a suppression of intertribal wars, but they represented a civilization in which mechanical warfare was a recognized institution of incredible destructiveness. A missionary had to be a saint to conquer so fully the ties of race and society that he would be able not to withhold from Africans the deepest parts of his cultural soul. There were some such saints—and indeed there are now—but they were understandably a small minority. Livingstone had no difficulty accepting tribal doctors as fellow professionals because he wanted to be so accepted by them, but there have been few Livingstones in the mission enterprise.

It is only saying that missionaries are human beings when their partial giving is described. It is only saying that Africans are human beings when their partial acceptance is described. No culture would be worth its salt that did not resist to some degree the invasions of another, no matter how many benefits and advantages the invasions might bring. Many Africans might, and many did, appreciate the value of Western religion, education and technology, but some were also bound to assert their dominion over how these values were to be organized in African life.

Separatist churches in Africa are the tangible outgrowths of the forces just described. They reflect the response of one total culture to another, for they mirror both what the missionaries brought and what the missionaries withheld, and they express the combined acceptance and resistance of Africans to this bringing and withholding. They are movements resembling the movements brought by the missionaries, but are uncontrolled by missionaries, and they are at some points directly hostile to notions stressed by missionaries. For all of these reasons, the separatist churches are frequently hostile to whites in general.

Separatist groups are so numerous and diverse that it is hard to generalize about them. Most of them are vigorously orthodox; many are fundamentalist in their use of the Bible; and some faithfully follow the Prayer Book of the Anglican Church. There are groups which combine pagan or Moslem practices with Christian ones, but these are at the fringes of separatism rather than at the heart.

The theory is widely held that the separatists broke away from the conventional denominations over the issue of polygamy, but this is erroneous. In some instances polygamy *was* a central cause of separation, but this was not so in far the greater number of cases. In general, the separatist bodies allow a greater latitude for polygamy than the mission churches, but there are wide differences of practice among them. Some are, if anything, even more rigid in their requirements of monogamy than their mission counterparts.

Sundkler felt that leadership frustration was one of the most crucial causes of separatism, and there can be no doubt that the prophetic or messianic leader looms large in the picture, yet there are numerous separatist churches in which the role of the clergy resembles that of Western-based institutions.

In South Africa, Sundkler distinguished two main types of separatists, and these he termed "Ethiopian" and "Zionist." The first reacted chiefly against racial discrimination; the second arose as a form of revivalism patterned after the independent denominations and churches of American Negroes. It is more than difficult, however, to maintain a clear distinction of this kind.

Take, for example, the East African movement known as The Society of the One Almighty God, which was launched toward the end of the last century by Joswa Kate Mugema. Himself a chief of considerable power and influence, he sought baptism as a Christian, when, among his own Uganda people, it was an exceedingly risky thing to do. He began to teach others to read the Bible, and in the course of his own avid studies he became more and more impressed with the story of the burning fiery furnace. If God could rescue men from a fire, He could also rescue them from sickness. Searching the Bible, Mugema found many examples of healing by faith.

Missionaries saw in him a man of deep piety and conviction, and he was licensed as a lay reader by the African Church Council. He was one of the first of the Anglican-converted chiefs to call for the abolition of slavery. He equipped expeditions for the evangelization of interior tribes. As a chief, he earned a reputation for great personal generosity, and he was a leader in placing before colonial administrators the grievances of his people. His individualism was reflected in his refusal to wear any head covering—because God had given him hair. He also ordered a square bed to be made for him "because he did not see why he should be forced to lie in any given direction."

Mugema's feelings about God, the Bible, and medicine

grew into an obsession. When attempts to persuade missionaries of the rightness of his views failed, he separated from the Church Missionary Society and formed a group of his own, the Bamalaki, or The Society of the One Mighty God. The sect grew rapidly both in numbers and in teachings, but the root of the new religion remained the objection to medicine for man or beast. There were in Buganda alone, by 1930, an estimated 56,952 Bamalakis. The congregations were grouped into local, county, and tribal councils, and then into a great All Churches Council. Clergy were formally ordained, and there was an official "prayer book." Several schools were established for Bamalaki children.

The society has now lost most of its influence over the younger generation and is definitely waning, but it still provides a fascinating case history of the rise, spread, and demise of an African separatist church.

A separatist movement that shows no present signs of diminishing strength is the United African Methodist Church, commonly called the Fishmonger Church, because its first building was near the Lagos fish market. The leaders of this group discovered that the fish was an early Christian symbol, and far from resenting the popular name for their schismatic effort, they have blazoned the emblem on their pulpits, literature, and the great brass cross which always precedes the bishop's processional.

The movement was triggered in 1917, when the chairman of the Methodist Mission in Lagos went on a crusade against polygamy. This was only the apparent rather than the real reason for the revolt, however, since monogamy is required of United African Methodist clergy and is encouraged among the laity. A genuine desire for independence was the underlying motive. Nationalist sentiments were rife in Nigeria even then, but there was little or no opportunity for their expression in politics.

The polity and liturgy of Methodism have been maintained through the years. Wesley's matins are read, and the hymns are those familiar to Western Protestants. But drums and native lyrics were introduced into the services, giving them a colorfully "African" flavor.

The United African Methodist Church is not growing to any appreciable extent; but its congregations are vigorous and enthusiastic, and they have status in the African community.

No one can travel much in West Africa without being struck by the ubiquitous Cherubim and Seraphim Societies. This flamboyant movement is neither dying nor static. It is flourishing. The principal founder was Moses Tunolashe, the son of a leading family of Ikare in western Nigeria. Like Mugema, he acquired an early prejudice against medicine, the beginning he was a maverick whose use of the Bible was but, unlike Mugema, he was never known to hanker after recognition by one of the established mission churches. From strictly his own.

He was told in an initial vision that he should found a society called Seraph. A subsequent vision added the word Cherub. Attracting followers from various churches, as well as from among traditional animists and Moslems, he adopted an appealing open-air type of evangelism, which is now common in the movement. Yet another vision revealed to Tunolashe that the Seraphim should wear white robes of a particular cut, and one of the profoundest strivings of his converts is the ability to afford their flowing cassocks.

The society has grown rapidly, to the great alarm of the settled churches. There is an anarchic, freewheeling quality to it, with a minimum of hierarchical administration, and a maximum of exotic, conglomerative practices. On entering their churches, Seraphim remove their shoes and cross themselves (an example of combined African, Biblical, Moslem, and Roman Catholic practices). There is a cross in the church, but no altar. Leaders, surrounded by candles and incense, carry a wooden or metal rod, which is variously used for sanctifying water, casting out demons, and leading the singing. Drums and bells are exuberantly employed in services, except during Lent, when they are strictly forbidden. Worship is periodically moved out of the church building to especially selected hilltops. The Bible is emphasized and Holy Week is a time of most solemn fasts, vigils, and observances; but just as much is made of dreams, visions, and mystical revelations.

Bewildering to those set in their accustomed denominational ways, the Cherubim have a deep appeal for many Africans in their "neither" world—that is, neither wholly African nor wholly Western—and especially for the unlettered multitudes moving into town and city life, who find little to excite them in the more formal churches, even when they are African-led, but who are impressed nevertheless with the prestige symbols of Bible, baptism, and cross.

What attitude to take toward these mushrooming separatist sects is a major problem for conventional Christian leadership, missionary and African alike. Catholics tend to assume that it is primarily a Protestant problem because there have been few organized secessions from the Roman fold, but this fails to take into account the thousands of individuals and families who defect from Catholicism to ally themselves with some separatist group.

Many of the sects come and go with stupefying rapidity, which is perhaps the separatist movement's gravest weakness. Still, new visionaries and "seers" are constantly arising to take the place of those who disappear, and some of the societies—the Cherubim, for example—possess remarkable staying powers. All, however, are isolated from the main stream of Christendom. They claim the name of Christ, but because of their variety and deviation from the Western norm they have no recognition but that of their own numbers.

In the separatist churches, many Africans find their own brand of the "freedom" in which they are "called in Christ." Their leaders are sometimes charlatans seeking nothing more than status or power—but only sometimes. The followers are seeking something substantial and lasting—community and a personal identity in a setting where they feel truly "at home." Is there any solution but to recognize that if the Church exists at all, it exists for each and every group that lays sincere claim to the name of Christ, whatever its detour from the accustomed Western paths?

Missionaries and an "Africanized" Church

On August 27, 1961, President Sékou Touré declared that the Government of Guinea intended to "Africanize" the Roman Catholic Church. "No Catholic prelate will be accredited to Guinea unless he is an African," Touré said. Just twenty-four hours before this announcement was made, Bishop Gerard de Milleville, a white French Catholic who had lived in Guinea for two decades, was expelled from the country.

This is but one more in a continuing line of flaring signals indicating that the Christian missionary enterprise in Africa is in serious trouble. Regardless of how valuable the missionary contribution to Africa has been, and might continue to be, the sentiment spreads among African leaders that the effort is no longer appropriate to their continent. "Missionaries should not feel despondent about this," say Africans. "The intellectual and religious loaves they have cast upon the waters have returned in the form of nationalism and our determination to run our own affairs. In that sense, missionaries have done their job well, and we thank them. Their devotion, including often enough even the sacrifice of their lives, has built schools and hospitals, and widened the horizons of our religious beliefs. Still they must go. Not that the needs of Africa in education, medicine, and spiritual growth are now met. Far from it! The point is that the missions as an institution in Africa must hand over the labors they initiated to other groups: on the one hand, to teams of international technicians who will work with African leaders; and, with respect to matters of the spirit, to prelates and pastors who are Africans. Missions, no less than colonial governments, must clearly understand the dimensions of change on this continent. They must not mistake the divine spark in their past work for divinity itself. Otherwise, more than missions will be in danger. The future of African Christianity will be jeopardized!"

One way to translate this sentiment is that the time for missions is over, but the time for African churches is still at hand. Christianity plays a universal role in the lives of men, but churches are rooted in communities and peoples. They are immediate, and their claims lay hold of the hearts of the people who are immediately in their midst. For this reason, missions, no matter how long established, must be temporary. Their inspiration stems from alien soil, and they are, therefore, as "out of phase" with current developments in Africa as colonialism is. They were, after all, linked with colonialism in the same historical process—the West's invasion of Africa. True though it may be that missionaries were often bitterly opposed to the policies of colonial officials and settlers; but the fact remains that the destinies of missions and colonialism have been locked together, and the end of one heralds the end of the other. To the extent that Africans have become, or wish to become, Christians, then to that extent Christian churches have a future in Africa. Africans must lead these churches, however, and must themselves determine the nature of their relations with world-wide Christianity and with their fellow Africans.

A political scientist, David E. Apter, of the University of Chicago, has tried to summarize the situation with these perceptive words:

> If African governments take over the tasks of training and development and if nationalism redresses the psychological imbalances of cultural change by rendering novelty harmless and integrating it with African society, what is left for religion? In the very efforts of nationalists to redress the balance of the past and to make large efforts to change their societies, it becomes increasingly difficult to cater to the personal needs of many of the ordinary men and women in Africa. Nationalism is a function of youth, not age. The young are in the nationalist movements, and nationalism is a phenomenon of young nations. But what of those who in their own personal lives struggle with both the meanings of changes wrought and adjustments to be made? For them churches can become new vital centers of thought. They can help to ameliorate some of the harsher effects of change. They can maintain the personality of individual men and the dignity of man as an individual. The danger is that human worth can be lost in the massive effort to redeem humanity as a whole. In this, churches can share with nationalists in the tasks that lie ahead, the one in catering to the individual, the other in catering to society as a whole. But this is not a task for missionaries.

Margaret J. Field, in her recent (1960) study of rural Ghana, *Search for Security*, offers some fascinating insights into the tasks facing African churches as missionary influence dwindles and as churches come to grips, on their own, with the spiritual problems of ordinary Africans.

The departure of missionaries from the scene will have little influence upon the religious beliefs of commonplace Africans, according to Dr. Field, because these beliefs have never really been deeply influenced by missionaries anyway. While it has been fashionable the world over for anthropologists to "deplore" the wrecking of tribal institutions by Christian missions, Dr. Field believes that this is "flogging a long-dead horse." She writes:

> Those anthropologists who thirty years ago were indignant at the ignorant misrepresentations of native religions by missionaries in different parts of the world may now, if they look around Ghana, witness the turning of the tables. Illiterate Africans have always been more shrewdly and critically reserved than either missionaries or anthropologists have suspected. The naïveté has been on the part of the foreigner. Christianity has always been the object of invidious observation by African pagans though courtesy and concrete self-interest have often forbidden criticism to be outspoken.

Her point is that Christian churches have a job cut out for themselves which cannot be fully measured until ordinary Africans have a chance to assess Christianity as an "African" rather than as an alien phenomenon. At present, skepticism about Christianity runs very high among pagan Africans. The chief point of criticism, remarkably enough, is that Christians are shamefully short of moral virtue! As long as Christianity is basically a foreign-dominated enterprise, it can be shrugged off as a strange but temporary aberration. But African churchmen, free of foreign overseers, have an intriguing vineyard in which to labor.

Dr. Field's long years in Ghana have convinced her that "So far as Africans think at all about creed, they see . . . no incompatibility between Christianity and paganism."

> Christians teach that God begat one son who still—on rather poor evidence in pagan eyes—works in and for his adherents. Pagans believe that God has many sons—all the *obosom* [gods]—who work for him most dramatically and convincingly. . . . Many

of the *obosomfo* [pagan priests] whose shrines I frequented are baptised Christians. One of them always wears a crucifix and has another surmounting the roof of his sanctuary. The first *obosomfo* at Mframaso not only founded a Christian school in his village but intended to build a church and in it to worship God every Sunday morning between his two sessions at the *obosom's* shrine. One of the present elders of the Mframaso shrine is also a pillar of a Christian church a few miles off, and does most of the organizing when the Bishop visits it. He is valued by both pagan and Christian communities for his good sense, fibre, fidelity and generosity. I asked him once why he, as a baptised Christian, became an elder of the *obosom's* shrine. He replied, with serene innocence, "Anyone can see that the *obosom* has power."

This, rather than a clear-cut ideological battlefield, is the blended realm in which the African church must work. Ordinary Africans, even modestly educated ones, do not suffer from the "split-mentality" of their elite brethren, according to Dr. Field. They suffer no agonies of feeling in being pulled apart by the tribal gods on one side and the precepts of Christianity on the other. Their reasons for joining Christian churches are varied. "But," says Dr. Field, "even the small proportion who join from a positive conviction of the superiority of the Christian faith and its consolations do not thereby embrace any belief in the *non-existence* of the gods they are ceasing to serve." Indeed, such converts customarily take farewell gifts to the sacred places of the old gods and explain that "they intend no offense and hope that none will be taken." These little ceremonies usually end with a promise by the convert that he has made arrangements with a responsible relative to take over his obligations to the *obosom.*

For the most part, illiterate and semiliterate African Christians continue to do their duties at the pagan shrines, and Dr. Field claims that she has even seen "training college teachers, lawyers, members of the Legislative Assembly, and some of the most highly educated men in the country" at *obosom* rites. Dr. Field concludes:

> It is quite true that Christian Church officers and employees—such as presbyters and school-teachers—when they consult shrines, go to distant ones and conceal their visits from their senior Christians, but this implies no conflict in their own minds, only a criticism of the missionary's abysmal ignorance of supernatural things. Not only does he lack understanding, he lacks the desire and capacity for it: therefore he must be humoured and deceived. But the African does not deceive himself, though he does, for prudential reasons, deceive those who can sack him or withdraw his scholarship. His own conscience needs no squaring and his own actions no rationalising.

It is intriguing to speculate on the future of African churchmanship as it reaches out to the needs of Africans *after* the "presence" of missionary supervisors is removed. What seems certain is that African churchmen will make much greater use of certain aspects of African religion and culture. No longer will this kind of *enrichment* be left to the separatist bodies. It is likely, for example, that Africans in the role of independent apostles to their own people will lay greater stress on God than on Christ as a starting point of Christian teaching. Christ does not fit easily into the African scheme of things, but the idea of a Supreme Being does. This does not imply that Christ will be ignored, but it does mean that an understanding of Christ will be drawn out of an understanding of God, rather than the other way around.

A second probable shift in emphasis will be development of the idea of the Supreme Being to cover the cult of the ancestors. Mission Christianity has shown precious little appreciation of the importance of African ancestral cults, yet they are the indissoluble bond of unity in African group life. As Shropshire said in *The Church and Primitive Peoples:*

"If Christianity cannot find a place for this worship then it has not yet found itself. . . ." It will be easier for mission-free African churchmen to find such a place for a force that nourishes in African life such primary virtues as love among members of a family and right behavior toward one's immediate fellows.

A third likelihood is a greater emphasis on agricultural festivals within a Christian framework. Africans are still primarily a rural and agricultural people. For the success of crops, they are deeply aware not only of the need for human skill and industry, but of a sense of harmony with the unseen world as well. African churchmen will almost certainly find places on their Christian calendars for ceremonials—including dancing and drumming—which bless the seeds at planting time and give thanks for the crops at harvest time. As one African Methodist leader expresses it: "This could very profitably replace that item which has haunted Methodist church calendars for a long time—Revival Sundays!"

A fourth lead was provided by the 1955 Conference on Christianity and African Culture in Accra. There it was decided that "the loss involved in the abolition of the ceremony [the traditional naming of a child] was too great, and that it should be retained, though modified by the substitution of Christian prayers for those addressed to the ancestors."

In connection with the "crisis" events of life—birth, marriage, and death—there is little doubt that "Africanized" Christianity will pay greater heed to natural African patterns. Baptism and the traditional naming of a child may well be associated, and with it an end brought to the mission custom of giving African children "Christian" names. All this ever did was put Christianity in a kind of separate compartment, anyway. If baptism and African "naming" are combined, there is no reason why it would not seem perfectly normal and devout to call upon an ancestor to "live again" in a child and endow it with his best qualities. There was a pertinent comment on this by one of my African Christian friends: "This would give a child a standard in later life to live up to. His baptism into the Christian fold just when he is entering 'the world of his ancestors' would be very appropriate."

A merging of African and Christian elements in wedding and funeral ceremonies will almost surely take place. For many years sensitive missionaries have been bothered by what they believed to be their obligation to disavow African marriages and burials done in the traditional fashion. African churchmen, on their own, are not likely to suffer from the inhibitions characteristic of their missionary mentors. In the words of an African Christian theologian, C. G. Baeta: "The setting, the external framework of these observances, should be taken directly from African Culture and be plainly reminiscent of it. But the meaning, the content, especially as expressed in words, should serve Christian purposes and provide Christian nurture. . . . The important thing is that for every occasion of heightened feeling there should be a custom combining African form and Christian content."

American Missionary Response

The sweep of African events has obviously forced missionaries into a precarious position. How are American missionaries responding?

John R. Gibson, a staff reporter for the *Wall Street Journal,* wrote from Southern Rhodesia in August, 1961:

> Like it or not (and many missionaries don't), they are being pressured to take sides on racial and political issues. Increasingly they are becoming identified in the minds of Africans as representatives of the U.S. instead of simply Christian workers above politics. And many of them are gradually giving up their old status of preacher-teacher-peacemaker for that of "technical ad-

visers" and counsellors to African churchmen and educators drawn from the native population. To adapt to these new circumstances, the missionaries are being tested, trained and re-evaluated as never before.

According to one dependable estimate, 15,970, or approximately 35 per cent of the world's 42,250 Protestant missionaries, are working in Africa. Since North American churches now dominate the mission scene, we can assume that they also account for the lion's share of Africa-based missionaries. The Missionary Research Library of New York reports that expenditures of U.S.-supported missions abroad have increased by 32 per cent in the past four years. Most of this has gone to Africa. The current rate of spending for overseas mission work by American Protestant bodies alone is about $170 million a year.

It is obvious that, from a missionary standpoint, Africa is the heart of the world. More than four hundred American church organizations sponsor some kind of missionary effort, while by comparison all of the State Department's embassies and consulates in Africa are staffed by only seven hundred American citizens. John Gibson reported that in Southern Rhodesia alone the number of different missions is so great that "the government has attempted to curb competition for souls by banning missions within five miles of each other."

If the missionary idea is really out of date for Africa, the American mission enterprise shows no present signs of reducing the tempo of its activities. What one does find, however, is a kind of nervous soul-searching, typified by Dr. Theodore L. Tucker, Executive Secretary, Africa Committee, Division of Foreign Missions of the National Council of Churches. At the University of Chicago seminar on *Changing Africa and the Christian Dynamic,* held in February, 1960, Dr. Tucker complained that missions and missionaries in

Africa could hardly be recognized from the descriptions of them given by many African spokesmen; yet he granted that "this is indeed what they sincerely hold and what they have seen while watching us work."

Tucker then said: "The widespread but inadequate idea of missions makes us ask ourselves this question. Doesn't the very word 'mission' have a suggestion of superiority and interference? Yet we might remember that the word is being used almost everyday in the secular press. There are diplomatic and trade missions, national and United Nations technical aid missions. What constitutes a 'mission' is not the people, nor the job, nor the place, but the fact that they have been sent. Any group of people possessed by an idea that they believe to be dynamic has a mission. Undoubtedly both the two great powers of our day, the United States and Russia, have this sense of mission.

"It is not unreasonable then that the Christian Church should also have a sense of mission. We believe ourselves to be part of the Church, which is God's own chosen instrument for saving the world, and achieving His purposes. . . .

"As Emil Brunner has said: 'The Church exists by mission, as the fire by burning.' Looking out on the world, the Church has no option but to evangelize. There is indeed a role for missionaries in Africa today, working within the Church's central task of mission."

Men like Tucker are fully aware of the Christian mission's uncertain future in Africa. They are keenly conscious of the new situation and of the changes in role and attitude which are required. They are by no means confident, but they are determined to keep on trying. They still list as the first two qualities needed by missionaries: A strong personal conviction with "personal knowledge of Jesus Christ," and a powerful capacity to interpret the Gospel. But next in line is a clear appreciation of the world in which the missionary lives. For

Africa, this means recognition of nationalism as the great issue, an ability to respond positively to the political interests of Africans, and a willingness to work under African direction. It means, too, a bold approach to the problems of racial relationship in multiracial areas.

"We also need to be aware," said Dr. Tucker, "of the changes brought by the growth of cities and of industry throughout Africa. While most of Africa is still rural, yet the urban areas are constantly increasing, and increasing in importance. Wherever the system of migrant labor is enforced, many of the adult males spend much of their time away from their families working in industries. By and large, our . . . missions have been geared to the rural areas and we have not made sufficient effort to seize the new opportunities of pioneering in the cities."

Another pioneering quality being encouraged in the African missionary is an understanding in depth of Islam as it is practiced south of the Sahara, not in the spirit of a crusade, but to know what is really involved in efforts to convert Africans from Islam to Christianity.

With the exception of some of the fundamentalist groups, recruitment of missionaries now includes elaborate psychological screening and testing to make certain that candidates can withstand a violent "culture shock" and are emotionally able to adjust to relationships with Africans. There are also increasing demands for bonafide technical skills, such as those possessed by Bruce Smalley, from Michigan, who is in charge of the experimental-farm program at Southern Rhodesia's Old Umtali Mission, and who knows at least as much about tractors, rabbit-breeding and crop rotation as he does about the Bible. He also knows how to work under an African "boss," the Rev. Kenneth Choto, the head man of Old Umtali, who shares G. Mennen Williams' partiality for bow ties.

Dr. Emory Ross, with forty years of missionary experience in Africa behind him, has put the American missionary response to Africa's nationalist turmoil in these ringing words:

> The real and heavy task, essential for Africa, for us, and for the world, is the creating of Christian Community in and with Africa —that Christian Community which is open not only to all peoples but which has concern for all of the life of all of the people. Land, food, clothing, shelter, health, religion, literacy, literature, education, communications, recreation, economics, family, community, government—all these things are, or should be, the Christian concern of Christians everywhere, for everybody. . . . For Christians, it is part of the life work of every generation, placed upon us by the teaching and example of Christ 2,000 years ago. . . . [It] is a service in which "oneness" is basic, for it must embrace the whole of man, the whole of life.
>
> [It] is a service which governments can never render in its entirety. It is a service essentially of peoples with peoples. . . . It is for educators and farmers, for economists and engineers, for doctors and writers, for artists and lawyers, for carpenters and musicians, for veterinarians and preachers and printers and motion picture people and editors. There are things to be done, at home and in Africa, by everybody. For this deals with the whole of life. It is peoples working with peoples for the good of all the people.
>
> There is nothing visionary and "do-goody" about this. It is one of the basic, solid facts of life. . . .
>
> Here is the time to advance. Here is the challenge for new Christian dynamism. . . .
>
> Africa has a pristine treasure. It is a sense of wholeness of life that comes, almost unaltered, from the primal days of man's creation. The West, too, has its treasures, some with vistas of joy and beauty so great that the soul is in agony to reach them. But wholeness in the West is nearly gone. . . .
>
> Christians can well say that Africa holds, direct from our Creator, some of the primal wholeness that we so widely seek. Let us join and aid her fully. With what we know, with what she has,

with what together we can as free men do, the world may well save its soul. . . .

Some indications that Dr. Ross' exalted hopes are not completely unfounded can be illustrated by scores of choice examples. I choose just one, that of Koinonia missionary Elizabeth Mooney, who went to Kenya to start a Literacy Center. During her first weeks in Nairobi, Miss Mooney felt like a doctor without patients. According to UNESCO, eight out of ten adults in Kenya cannot read or write, but where, she kept asking herself, were the illiterates?

She had picked Nairobi for her main effort because she thought it would be easier in the capital city to contact prospective students; but she had not reckoned with the suspicion that greeted announcements by government publicity vans that Miss Mooney was available for literacy lessons. She discovered only later that most Nairobi Africans thought it was a scheme to raise more taxes or an excuse to move them out of the city to some back-country area. As the weeks rolled by, she tried handbills, posters, and radio announcements. Still no students, no teachers, and no staff.

Finally—and Miss Mooney believes it was in answer to her prayers—she met Dr. Gikonyo Kiano, a Ph.D. from Stanford. He was teaching economics at the Royal Technical College of Nairobi, and had heard Frank Laubach speak in the United States. He listened carefully to Miss Mooney and agreed to recruit voluntary teachers for her. "Many old men helped me to get my education," he said, "now I will be helping many old men to get their education."

Dr. Kiano spent his month-long vacation talking to African groups. He found that the people thought the literacy program would divert funds needed for building more schools for their children. He explained that this was a "self-help" program and that within six months an adult could become literate and would then be better able to aid his children and community. His words were accepted and trusted. He broke the ice by finding the first twenty teachers, and within four months there were three hundred enrollees in the Nairobi classes. Then came the real breakthrough! Miss Mooney went to an African political rally and gave a brief description of her program. The Criminal Investigation Department of Kenya's then colonial government promptly informed her that she had committed a blunder. But Tom Mboya himself had invited her to speak and acted as her translator. Her "blunder" turned out to be the best move she had made in Africa. Within a week, enrollment in literacy classes tripled. The program spread like a brush fire from Nairobi to the villages of Kenya, where the overwhelming majority of the country's two and a half million illiterates live.

Moral Re-Armament: Hoax or Hope?

Frankly I have been amazed at the number of times Americans have asked me what I thought of Moral Re-Armament's work in Africa. Many people apparently read Moral Re-Armament's pamphlets, newsletters, magazines, and full-page advertisements in which there are routine claims to great and transforming "good works" by MRA task forces operating among Africans.

For those who do not know, Moral Re-Armament is a movement about four decades old, which was founded by Dr. Frank N. D. Buchman, an ordained Lutheran minister. In August, 1961, Dr. Buchman died. The future of the organization he initiated and dominated is uncertain, but by the time of his death it had extended its well-financed operations around the globe. The number of Buchman's followers is unknown since there are no membership lists or congregations. Buchman consistently claimed a Christian title for his movement, but MRA literature is notably short of theological language. Some of the very important people, past and present, who have publicly indicated their support of MRA are Gen. John J. Pershing, Henry Ford, Admiral William H. Standley, Konrad Adenauer, Norman Vincent Peale, Richard Nixon, and Mae West.

In personal terms, MRA preaches the virtue of four Absolutes: honesty, purity, unselfishness and love. In its public information program, the movement consistently stresses the notion that only MRA has an ideology capable of coping successfully with Communism: "The choice for the world is Moral Re-Armament or Communism." In recent years, MRA's literature has claimed a considerable role in stemming the tide of Communism in Africa.

I was unable to uncover any of MRA's "miracles" in Africa, but I did run into a good many reactions, most of them hostile. Handouts have made much of a statement attributed to President Kasavubu of the Congo to the effect that MRA has "found the secret of liberation for Africa." And use has repeatedly been made of a speech delivered in 1949 by Nnamdi Azikiwe. The setting was MRA's lavish complex of hotels and inns at Caux, Switzerland. Azikiwe spoke warmly of the "wonderful experience at Caux," and paid tribute to MRA as "an island of peace and harmony in a sea of discord." But whatever initial impression Moral Re-Armament made on this veteran Nigerian nationalist-politician, he recently lodged a complaint against the unauthorized use of his name in MRA literature. The June 3, 1961, issue of *West Africa* carried this report: "I was glad to see Dr. Azikiwe's dignified complaint against the misuse of his name by Moral Re-Armament in a full-page advertisement the movement wanted to insert in all Nigerian newspapers (some spotted this and refused the advertisement, which was a little less expensive than the 1,000 pounds or more MRA pays for pages in the

London *Times*). The Governor-General who was not consulted in any way, was alleged to have declared that he had found at the MRA headquarters at Caux an idea which 'proved to be a pearl of great price,' but he protested that MRA was using his name for its own selfish interests. It has, in fact, done so for years; and I wonder if the Deputy Prime Minister of Sierra Leone, also quoted in the advertisement, had been consulted?"

Complaints about MRA tactics are not always this mild or poised. Here, for what they are worth, are some of the more typical responses of Africans:

MRA is a passing phenomenon in Africa. Like other ideas now pouring into Africa it will be challenged by nationalism and especially by Pan-Africanism. Their days are numbered, and it will not be long before this phony, treacherous, imperialist organization is kicked out of Africa.

People who spend their funds on MRA are suckers, and those Africans who turn to MRA are suckers too. The whole operation is a crack-pot business. Western Governments should wake up to the activities of MRA in African countries. They may wake up too late to discover that MRA has done more harm than good. MRA is bound to complicate the administration of America's foreign policy in Africa. I often wonder why American capitalists should be so foolish. Don't they realize that they would do more good to the peoples of undeveloped countries if they were to spend their money on concrete projects of economic and social development than waste it on young neurotics who seek adventure and excitement in the name of saving others from moral depravation and Communism?

Africans who accept MRA sponsorship and allow themselves to be transported around and shown-off are acting opportunistically. Their behavior can be explained. It is understandable, even though opportunism of any sort, ideally, should be repudiated. But what else can one expect when MRA itself is so guilty of opportunism? When it encourages it? When its supporters are equally opportunistic?

Yes, I took the MRA's money. I let them fly me to their World Assembly, and to the United States. I made all the nice speeches they wanted me to make. I'm getting old. How else could I have gotten to see the world? But I hope our young people will not be allowed to get mixed up with this group. It does not promise us any good. It can only add to the confusion in Africa today.

I see where President [William] Tubman is being quoted in MRA literature about how MRA is the best way to get unity and freedom for Africa. What else was he expected to say? Don't all decent men and women proclaim these general principles?

So, they are trying to arm us Africans morally. Does this mean they believe Africans to be immoral? It's the same stuff all over again. If there are people who need to be morally re-armed, they are the people in the West. What is MRA doing in Mississippi and Alabama?

Readers of MRA publications are bombarded with repetitive stories about African personalities who, in partnership with MRA task forces, are reputed to be performing miracles of reconciliation and anti-Communism. These personalities are named, pictured and described as "a former Mau Mau leader," "a Ghanaian colonel," "a leading Nigerian nationalist," "a prominent Congolese patriot," etc. It is simply impossible to document or confirm these descriptions. The "former Mau Mau leader" is not known to Kenyans as a former leader of any kind. The "leading Nigerian nationalist" is not recognized as such by other Nigerians. And so it goes.

MRA movies are from time to time shown to African audiences, and some MRA programs have been broadcast over African radio stations. Groups of Africans do make, and break off, relationships with MRA "missionaries" and photographers. One MRA man, Dr. William T. Close, an American surgeon, has worked devotedly, without pay, in an East Leopoldville hospital. He is written about in virtually every issue of MRA literature, but he is apparently the only one of his kind, for there are no similar stories.

It was Frank Buchman's claim that his movement was "all out for God." Without disputing it, there is still the necessity of saying that Africa most assuredly is not all out for Moral Re-Armament. As a Christian influence in Africa, MRA is at best negligible; at worst a source of irritation.

Is It To Be "Thank You, Now Goodbye"?

Anyone would be beyond his depth who tried to predict Christianity's future in Africa. Missionaries are being expelled from Guinea, Sudan, and Somaliland; but these are only three out of very many present or future African states. Whether or not the new nationalism will sweep missionaries out of additional countries is impossible to foresee, but the mood explored in the next chapter offers some badly needed insight into a bit of history-in-the-making which is largely ignored among us.

The Christian Century of January 4, 1961, carried these somber and relevant reflections by the Wake Forest religious scholar, G. McLeod Bryan:

> It may well be that as far as Western Christianity's influence on what is happening in Africa is concerned we will have to be satisfied with the indirect approach which was effected by the bringing of the Bible, by the planting of the idea of freedom, and by the educating of their leaders. The direct means of shaping African political events seem to be gone. And from the mood described herein, a mood which is every bit as much a part of the current scene as the Uncle Tomism involved in missions, we can expect a sizable element in the indigenous Christianity to join the hue and cry for national institutions, including the churches. This may mean that all that missions will receive from their well-meaning friends as well as from self-confident nationalist leaders is a mere "Thank you, now goodbye."

Wistfully we are prone to listen to the hopeful voices with regard to the future of missions in Africa. Unfortunately, these voices may be those of compliant leaders of local churches and societies, created in part by the missionary attitude, rather than those of the policy-makers of the new nation-states. This is no alarmist warning, but a sober reminder that we cannot ignore the background of the church's present setback in Africa.

VI

Attitudes of the African Elite Toward Religion

"In the very near future Christianity is going to lose out in Africa. It is already losing out. Do you think that I am returning to Africa to remain a Christian? No! Karl Marx was right when he said, 'Religion is the opium of the people.' Religion is holding us back. Our people continue to sing, clap, and pray, but Christianity is losing because it is a crutch, and when the crutch can no longer support you, it should be put aside. Of course, Christianity may continue to have an appeal for the poor classes who find time to indulge in fantasies. They have no effective outlets; they have no real intellectual life or material wealth for fruitful diversions —traveling, going to movies or theaters, and giving parties or being entertained by others. Religion is for them the only source of contemplation. For the educated class, religion has no value."

These dogmatic assertions came in response to the simple question: What future do you see for Christianity as the religious commitment of Africa's rising elite? The speaker is a Nigerian in his late thirties, married and the father of two. He has been a Methodist for as long as he can remember, and he taught for some years in a mission school before coming to the United States to do graduate work. Back home he had been a licensed lay preacher and occupied numerous pulpits. He replied to the question without the slightest hesitation, even though he was aware that his answer was being recorded verbatim, and no explanation had been given of the question's purpose.

He went on to say, with a broad smile, that he had not missed a Sunday service during his stay in the United States, where he has been attending a Negro college in a small eastern Pennsylvania town. Before his departure for the United States, Methodist leaders in Nigeria had given him introductory letters to Methodist leaders here. He first tried to attend the Methodist Church in the college town. The all-white congregation discouraged him from doing so, and indicated that he would not be welcome as a member.

With admirable curiosity, he checked into the matter and discovered that Pennsylvania was the very state in which the African Methodist Episcopal Church was founded in 1786 by Richard Allen and his associates. The reason: religious estrangement and humiliations endured because of segregation in a Philadelphia Methodist Church. The result: the spread of separate Negro churches in the United States.

After being snubbed by the local church, he traveled a considerable distance each Sunday to attend the Negro Methodist Church closest to the college. This congregation, he said, was thirty-nine miles away, and the round-trip bus fare averaged $4.00 each Sunday, exclusive of donations to the church. He has a sense of loyalty toward the Methodist Church, in spite of his hostile attitude toward Christianity's future in Africa. His experience with American ecclesiastical segregation is, however, embittering. In his general views on Christianity he makes no particular distinction between Protestantism and Catholicism, though he does feel a preference for Methodism.

When pressed to explain why he thinks Christianity has such a poor future in Africa, he criticized missionaries and African church leaders. He said: "The white missionaries who come to Africa for evangelism have not yet Christianized their own people. They should first see the beam in their own eyes before that in their neighbors. Missionaries should not go to Africa to blindfold the people. I cannot understand why there should be segregation in the Church. The Church is a business, and it is not encouraging to see the wealthy [!] and well-fed missionaries, and their bootlicking African ministers, collecting money from the poor. If anything, African-controlled churches are even worse; they are certainly money-making organizations for the benefit of the leaders."

As his thoughts flowed on, he became even more inconsistent: "I prefer Methodism. It is to me another club to which you belong. I believe in peace of mind. In the Church I find an opportunity to contemplate. I feel relieved whenever I can discuss my problems with a minister. I believe in the existence of God. I do not believe either in Heaven or Hell. I do not know about either's existence. Ministers and missionaries make out too much about Hell. I believe that there is a Being than can answer our prayers. I do not believe in spirits and they have no meaning for me."

He has rejected, apparently, the relevance of *teme,* the unseen spirit world, which, as we have recorded, is of such crucial importance in traditional African beliefs.

This Nigerian spoke passionately and with deep conviction when he attacked the Church, the missionary enterprise, and religion in general. Yet he is clearly ambivalent. On the one hand, there is an ill-concealed wish to see the entire Christian movement liquidated in Africa; on the other, there are mellow personal associations with Christian worship and the ministry.

Do these sentiments have any significance? I record them because they are characteristic of a substantial segment of the rising African elite, a class that consists of educated professional men and women, teachers, and intellectuals. It is still a tiny class in most African countries, and it includes both those who have completed only secondary school and those with university training. Some of its members have had less formal education, among them journalists, trade union leaders, and prominent politicians; but by reason of their own efforts they belong quite rightly to the intellectual elite. They are Africa's opinion-makers, Africa's face to the world.

Within the elite are many professing and practicing Christians, but when they are confronted with such views as those expressed by the Nigerian they become apologetic and defensive. They will defend Christian ideals, but they are unlikely to defend the Church and missionaries with a passion equal to that of attackers. This is a serious weakness of the Christian believers among the rising African elite. In some ways it is more detrimental to the mission of Christianity in Africa than the attacks of detractors.

If this is a general rule, however, there are notable exceptions. The Southern Rhodesian nationalist, Ndabaningi Sithole, has written fulsomely of Christianity's role in Africa: "The Christian Church, by sending religious, educational and industrial missions to Africa has broadened the outlook of many an African; it has provided opportunities for many Africans to develop their latent qualities, and it has discouraged tribal hatreds and encouraged universal brotherhood instead. In many ways the Christian Church has provided Africa with sound political leadership. The present enlightened African political leadership would be next to impossible but for the Christian Church that spread literacy to many parts of Africa."

Sithole has his counterparts among the African elite. Others would be much more reserved. Still others would call Sithole's words "the sentimental apologia of a stooge."

A few years ago, the Institute of African-American Relation (now the African-American Institute, Inc.) conducted an essay competition for African students in the United States. The purpose of the project was to elicit the views of young Africans on strengthening African-American relations, and the Institute reports that forty students, undergraduate and graduate, entered the competition. Geographically, the students were distributed as follows: Nigeria (25), Liberia (4), Ghana (3), South Africa (2), Uganda (2), Southwest Africa (1), Cameroons (1), Northern Rhodesia (1), and Kenya (1).

Because the students had a great deal to say about missionary Christianity, their papers constitute one of the few existing broad surveys of elitist African religious sentiment.

A Liberian wrote: "One of the greatest, if not the greatest, benefits which Africa was received [sic] from the United States is the work of her missionaries. They have gone to all parts of the continent and have established churches, schools, and hospitals. . . . Had it not been for these missionaries, education in many parts of the continent would not have advanced as it is today."

A student from Uganda expressed a similar opinion: "Perhaps the most harmonious and most deeply penetrating relations between Africa and the United States have been effected through the work of non-governmental agencies such as missions, educational institutions, philanthropic foundations. . . . There is no doubt in our minds as to the sincerity and devotion of Americans toward Africa and other parts of the world in this respect."

However, some who were quite ready to credit the contributions of missionaries were also highly critical: "Well-meaning missionaries, who go to Africa," a Nigerian student stated, "put emphasis on the fact that Africans are poor, and thereby try to collect money at home to help Africa. . . . It would be much better if they would rightly emphasize the fact that Africans are poor because they are deprived by exploitation and domination, of the natural resources and wealth of their continent."

Another student described missionaries as "agents of misrepresentation abroad," and said they were "wolves in sheepskins." Along the same caustic lines, a student wrote that missionaries are guilty of "more sensational falsehood than ever to draw people into mission work."

A Nigerian, playing on this theme, charged that missionaries discouraged other organizations from operating in Africa: "The foreign missions in Africa which have contributed toward development often stand in the way of other agencies coming out to Africa. It is a pity the way some missionaries go home and tell horrible tales with the object of raising funds for extended work in Africa. Though they generally get the desired public response financially, nevertheless the repercussions which such tales produce falsify the impressions of the Africans among the peoples in the foreign countries. Some other organizations are, therefore, discouraged indirectly from going out. It would have been much appreciated if such missionaries were more diplomatic in the creation of their tales."

The American image of Africa has unquestionably been distorted for the reasons these students describe. Violence, misery, and primitivism are gambits too tempting to be resisted by some missionaries in their reports to the congregations back home. The issue has importance because it is interpreted so broadly by certain Africans. They see in it a revelation of how essentially well-meaning persons—in this instance, missionaries—can fall into the trap of ignoring the relevance of means to the ends they are pursuing.

African reasoning follows these lines: The gross exaggerations by missionaries of the conditions of African life are calculated to elicit the sympathy of home congregations for continued evangelism. The technique of degrading the African people is regrettable, but it does justify support for many necessary works of redemption. This same technique functions, however, at an irrational level. The missionary, by virtue of his religious convictions, assumes his superiority over those who do not share his convictions; and in his relations with Africans, the missionary's assumption reinforces itself through the very process of missionary work. He takes pleasure in bringing to Africans what he has been conditioned to feel is superior to what Africans have. The sense of superiority is thoroughly cloaked in feelings of moral and religious uprightness.

There are Africans who are brutally frank about this. Said one: "I am not sure most missionaries can rationally distinguish between the dualism of their motives, and it may well be that psychoanalysis would reveal more than they are willing to admit. Their supporters and sponsors at home have long been accustomed to the vicarious thrills of African mission field reports. Many an African student in the United States and Europe will tell you what he has seen in churches in this connection. I remember instances myself. Not too long ago a pair of Nigerian girls studying in a church-supported school came to me with tears in their eyes. They said I had 'to do something about it.' (I was then Executive Secretary of the All-African Student Union of the Americas.) The two girls had been at a church program where slides on Nigeria were shown. The missionary introduced his audience to Nigeria with a slide which had a monkey on it. This was the first slide, and, according to the two girls, it purported to symbolize the origins of the Nigerian people. The slides which followed depicted life among the Tiv people in Northern Nigeria. To this day, many Tiv wear very scanty clothes, and, I believe, hides and leaves. The girls told me that nothing else was shown about Nigeria, and they thought I should protest officially to the group. The experience was enough to sour their attitude toward missionaries and, indeed, toward Christian missions in Africa."

In the papers written for the Institute, several students criticized missionaries for assuming the role of martyrs, who had given up their creature comforts back home in order to live and work among virtual savages. A student from Kenya commented: "It impresses many natives to hear of the good country and the many facilities for living which these missionaries have sacrificed in America in order to go and live with them."

Obviously there is an element of truth underlying this. Missionaries *do* make many personal sacrifices, but a thoughtful African would assume that they knew what they were doing in accepting their mission. In another sense, the claim of personal sacrifice produces amusement among Africans. A favorite topic of conversation among Africans after the Congo began to settle down was that the same missionaries who had fled screaming rape and murder were remarkably anxious to return.

A Nigerian student wrote: "I remember one American mission which the English civil servants often complained about. The American mission had its own colony, a self-constituted and privileged enclave. They lived in excellent houses and drove the biggest and latest-model cars. Compared with the English civil servants, their standard of living was immeasurably higher. Compared with the Africans, the missionaries lived in paradise. All in all, they lived in opulence. Their premises were as inaccessible to an uneducated African communicant as the army barracks. In part, the English administrators were jealous. On the other hand, I believe that they were voicing legitimate criticism. In my judgment, the administrators with whom I worked were a much better breed of human beings than the missionaries I knew. This is a harsh judgment, but I have heard many Africans who had close contacts with white missionaries complain bitterly of their exclusiveness and arrogance."

Another student complained about the way in which missionaries encouraged and accepted "gifts" of fruit, meat, and other things from their congregations. He wrote: "It is true that Africans are generous people and that we express our generosity through gifts. Unfortunately the missionaries had practically transformed this practice into an obligation. In fact, this practice was extended to mission elementary schools. I remember when my brother used to come back from school and asked my parents to buy him eggs so that he could take them to school because some important church official was visiting. My father complied on more than one occasion and then had to put a stop to it. I think, the practice was discontinued at this particular school. However, the more far-reaching consequence of this practice was that lower-level African clergy and lay workers went a step ahead of the missionaries and transformed this practice into a form of 'dash' or outright bribery for one or another favor done."

Even those who praised the work of missionaries were often critical of their attitude toward African culture. A student from Uganda commented: "They . . . required converts to give up customs and traditions without which life lost meaning. They have been guilty of cultural arrogance, a self-centered approach towards the Africans whom they considered as doomed pagans." He scored missionaries for making no distinction in their teaching between "purely religious ideas and merely social attitudes."

When this point was reviewed with a sophisticated African, he observed that many missionaries did indeed act as if they were obeying the dictum of Professor Diedrich Westermann, the German Christian anthropologist, who admonished: "However anxious a missionary may be to appreciate and to retain indigenous social and moral values, in the case of religion he has to be ruthless. . . . He has to admit and even to emphasize that the religion he teaches is opposed to the existing one and the one has to cede to the other."

The difficulty here is that few Westerners can be certain which African idea is "religious" (in a Western sense), and which constitutes a social and cultural attitude! As expressed by a perceptive African: "The conflict of Christianity with African social and cultural life is perhaps the most serious issue for the Church in Africa. It is precisely at this point that African leadership is called for in the Church, for they must be prepared to compete both with traditionalists and with our rising elite and intellectuals to show cause why we should abandon our way of life in favor of Christianity. Here Christianity faces and will continue to face grave difficulties as African nationalism develops its own myths and ideas about the nature of things, of society, and of Nature itself."

It is significant that several of the students in the Institute competition called for a rapid transfer of mission leadership to African hands if further suspicion was to be avoided. A Liberian contributor voiced approval of tendencies in this direction and cited the Roman Catholic Church as "the first to catch the vision and put into practice African church leadership."

But when another African was confronted with this statement, he said: "Obviously, this fellow does not realize the monolithic character of Catholic leadership and the difficulties which many countries have experienced in their relationship to the hierarchy in Rome. In fact, this difficulty has reared its head. At a very personal level, I remember losing an intimate African friend, who has since completed his training for the Catholic priesthood, because we disagreed on political matters and the tactics employed by the Catholic Church. Our controversy started when my friend wrote to me lauding the actions of the Catholic Youth Association for having been instrumental, through what I considered to be acts of hooliganism, in breaking up a political rally for a candidate which the Catholic clergy had disapproved. I wrote to him citing how dangerous it would be for the very survival of the Church in Africa if its leaders were to engage in obstructionist politics. I never heard from my friend since then. I have, however, been informed that he himself has become quite bitter toward the political activities of the Catholic clergy."

Members of the African elite are generally firm in calling for a divorce of organized religion from politics. Some say that the record of Christian missions, with their "political dealings, compromises, and outright betrayals of African rights," has made them keenly anxious to keep the two domains separate. There is a widespread feeling, for example, that the Catholic Church was involved in intrigues against the Congo government of Patrice Lumumba. Sentiment prevails that religious diversity is so great in many African countries that the separation of institutional religion from state affairs is a practical necessity. It is feared that wherever religion becomes a political issue, the old specter of a divided and fragmented Africa is strengthened. Something of this kind was in the mind of western Nigeria's leading political figure, Chief Obafemi Awolowo, when he wrote in 1947:

> . . . the Government [British Administration] of Nigeria has all along helped to keep the flame of this [Moslem religious] fanaticism burning brightly. . . .
>
> There was a time when the Government forbade Christian missionaries to propagate the Gospel in the Northern Provinces. Even now they operate only within limited areas. The ostensible explanation for this policy was that it would hurt the religious susceptibilities of the Moslem North. And it is argued that this might react unfavourably on the conduct of political affairs there. In the eyes of the Northerners, those who live in Southern Nigeria, unless they are Moslems, are styled "Kaferis" [Pagans] no matter if they are Christians. And because they are "Kaferis" they are looked upon with contempt and revulsion. At the conference of the Northern Chiefs in 1942 a letter written by the West Africa Students' Union in London came up for discussion . . . and the writers appealed to the Northern Emirs and their people for cooperation with those in the South in tackling these problems. The Emirs' comment on this appeal for cooperation, as contained in the official report of the conference is as follows: "Holding this country together is not possible except by means of the religion of the Prophet. . . . If they want political unity let them follow our religion."

With the realities of independence upon them, the Emirs and people of northern Nigeria have changed their political tactics if not their religious philosophy. They are living together with "Kaferis" in a united, free Nigeria. But it is not difficult to imagine the strife awaiting a Nigeria in which religious groups actively sought special influence and privilege.

It is this possibility which led a Nigerian student to call for the abolition of all religious schools. "I am not," he said, "for religious supported schools in Nigeria. You can't have two masters. All the religions seek converts and they find the schools to be fair channels for recruiting new members. The separation must be complete. They must not interfere with the education of youth. Why should we suffer double taxation: the state taxes for education and religious bodies tax their congregations for private schools. Besides, most of these church-supported schools are badly run. There are too many denominations. There are too many and diverse standards; too many philosophies of education; entirely too many principles of education. We need complete government direction of the education of our youth. If we do not, then we shall continue to produce young people educated in the image of Europe or the white world as a whole. There is too much wrong with education as it is now and we must revamp the whole thing if we are to produce the 'African personality.' "

The same point was given a more violent twist by another student: "The chief evil of Christian evangelism in Africa has been its psychological legacy. Christianity is the religion of our oppressive foreign masters. Its further propagation among a people who are trying to shake off the yoke of their foreign masters may be looked upon with suspicion. The idea of trying to persuade the black man to accept the white man's God is nothing but synonymous to persuading him to accept his role of inferiority."

This last expression, as irrational as it may sound, is crucial for understanding the nettles Africa's rising elite feel when they reach for Christianity as a possible religious commitment. For a member of the elite, the problem shapes itself in this way. It is quite correct to say that Christian influences molded, in varying degrees, the thinking of older African political leaders. Their generation depended almost exclusively on mission schools for education at virtually all levels, and there has remained among them a reservoir of good will for the missionary enterprise. Thus, the generation that first took Africa's political reins in its hands criticized the Church and some of the practices of Christianity, but with a tempering sense of sympathy and personal obligation.

At a speech delivered in 1957 at the Centenary Celebrations of the Niger Mission of the Church Missionary Society, the then fiery nationalist leader, Dr. Nnamdi Azikiwe, felt free to offer this flowery tribute:

> Your Grace, my main task was to assure you and our distinguished guests that the objective of the Church Missionary Society in this diocese has been achieved. The Society has been sending evangelists, teachers and physicians to teach us, to preach to us, to heal our physical infirmities, and to baptize us so that we may experience a new life in a new society that would be Christocentric. The seed which these evangelists with a mission had sown has yielded fruits of which the society should be proud. . . . Your Grace, I am happy to join in amplifying and broadcasting this historic achievement after one hundred years of sacrifice, of martyrdom, and of faith in the future of humanity. This is a modern miracle. Indeed, the Christian community is a fellowship of the brave who live by faith. Otherwise, would the sixteen clergymen and the nine laymen who founded the Church Missionary Society 158 years ago, have dreamt dreams and seen visions of a Nigeria redeemed from the thraldom of superstition and transformed into a citadel of Christianity barely a century after the landing of the *Dayspring* at Onitsha? Your Grace, "This is the Lord's doing, and it is marvellous in our eyes."

There are many in Azikiwe's generation, but far fewer in the next, who are willing to witness in such glowing terms to the "miracle" of Christianity in Africa. The younger leaders and intellectuals are more reluctant to praise and readier to criticize. They are likely to speak in a detached way of Christianity's future chance in Africa, saying that it will depend on "the intellectual leadership of Christian believers among Africans," and "on their performance and integrity as 'good' human beings."

Youthful African intellectuals insist that Christians can no longer point to the record of achievement or performance of foreign missionaries for "selling" their religion to the rising elite. One reason for this is the belief among many young intellectuals that they can discover alternative sources of intellectual, moral, and ethical life, which are independent of Christianity's Western bias, although similar values may be shared by Christians in many parts of the world.

Such alternative satisfactions are unlikely to lead them toward a Christian commitment in the same sense that the generation of Nyerere and Azikiwe was committed. As long as the Christian Church had a near monopoly of the education of Africans, and also of such essential services as hospitals, the men and women whom they trained, or who enjoyed these services, were inclined to react generously toward the Christian faith. However, since these services can now be increasingly obtained outside the religious community, there is a different psychological situation.

The Elite Sense of History

"The evil men do, lives after them. The good is oft interred with their bones." Substantially, this describes what is happening in the religious thinking of many of the younger elite. It may be no more than a temporary reaction, but for the time being, it prevails. The record of contact with Europeans is the most vivid and immediate "history" African intellectuals possess. This record is their point of departure in trying to make sense of their particular situation in the contemporary world.

African youth meetings are almost ritualistic in their obsession with the notion that Africans were the last peoples enslaved in recent history, that the Christian Church at the highest levels saw no contradictions in the exploitive acts of its countrymen, and that the continuing oppression of the

Negro in the United States remains a hated evidence and monument of this humiliation.

Ayo Ogunshaye, Director of Extra-Mural Studies at University College, Ibadan, has denounced this obsession of young Africans as a "slavery complex." He advises getting rid of it as quickly as possible, but he is bucking a powerful tide which has by no means run its course.

At a conference of African students in the United States, held at the University of Chicago in 1958, Dr. Alexander Ohin of Togoland told the delegates:

The discovery and colonization of the Americas by the Spaniards coincided with the Renaissance when the power of money was really above everything else. Missionaries who followed the Conquistadors were unable to protect the aborigines against ruthless exploitation. Las Casas, the most famous of them, traveled several times to Europe in attempts to denounce to Madrid the abuses of the colonists. . . . His compatriots even almost lynched him and he was accused of being a crypto-Lutheran.

On the other hand, active efforts were made to use the missionaries not on behalf of Christianity, but in the service of colonization and slavery. Archives of the colonies are extremely significant on this particular point. . . . Religion, said the King of France, is necessary for all men, but it is more necessary in the colonies populated with slaves which cannot be contained but by the hope of a better life . . . "after death." Under the Restoration, the Minister of the Navy wrote to the Governor of Martinique: "The missionaries must realize how dangerous it would be, while explaining too extensively the wise maxims of the Gospel, to preach equality which is in opposition with the constitutive principle of colonization" . . . Napoleon I, at the session of the Conseil d'Etat on May 22, 1804, said: "My intention is to re-establish the Maison des Missions Etrangers; those religious men will be much helpful to me in Asia, Africa, and America. I will send them to gather information about the countries. Their robes protect them and hide any economical or political intention."

Dr. Ohin made it clear to the students that he knew personally many missionaries, Protestant and Catholic, who did not compromise their principles. His theme was not personal but "historical," a theme that is now calculated to impress young Africans more powerfully than all the "good" individual missionaries have achieved. It may be a "slave-mentality" approach to history, but the impact is real on the mind of Africa's rising elite. For the present, it is their bitter heritage, and it is likely to be further elaborated in the school curriculum of the independent countries.

London was the scene of the 1960 Conference of All African Students in the United Kingdom, East and West Europe, the United States, and Africa. The theme of Christianity's historical association with slavery, colonialism, imperialism, and racism rose like bile in virtually every delegate's speech. One of the most passionate addresses was that of B. Chango Mackyo, who represented the East and Central African Students Union in the United Kingdom:

> Practically every nation has laughed at us. We have been scorned by both big and small nations. We have been subjected to contempt; we have known every form of abuse, humiliation and beastly ill-treatment from the so-called "Christian civilized world!" Friends, next to the beast of burden, the African is the most patient animal. We have turned the other cheek, but this has never been appreciated! We have sung, whistled and laughed in our sorrows, but this human behavior has had no effect on our tormentors! Instead we have been called fools, stupid niggers who are devoid of human feelings, who have no human values and who are nothing but half-beasts! Millions of our people were carried to slavery with the approval of even the highest religious authorities! The profits from the African slaves built castles, churches, cities. . . . This may sound like history, but slavery is still with us to this day! In South Africa, in Southern Rhodesia, Angola, and Mozambique the black man's lot is one of extreme suffering and untold misery. We are all slaves because millions of

our people are still suffering from the humiliating state of foreign political, economic and spiritual domination.

Younger African leaders and intellectuals, unlike their predecessors of a generation ago, are assailed by wide-ranging stimulations from the mass media. Abuses are broadly framed. The behavior of "Christian" nations in Africa is an *ideological* as well as a local and personal matter. Christianity is attacked for these abuses in ideological terms, and the attack is backed by a detailing of "hypocrisies." G. M. J. Cabral gave the students at the London Conference this heated account of mission activities in Portuguese African possessions:

> There are practically no schools, or rather some schools in the hands of the Catholic Church, and do you know, to teach what? Not the love of God, but the love of Portugal. All Catholic missionaries, though they are not called civil servants . . . are held to be personnel "in the special service of national and civilizing utility." These are the actual words of the missionary statute of 1941. Mission work in the colonies is subsidized by the Government.

Luis D'Almeida of "Mouvement Populaire de Liberation de l'Angola" took the floor to add his own caustic account of conditions in Angola:

> It is often the case that instead of attending courses, the [African] children are taken to work in the mission farms or plantations, without knowing anything about reading or writing. . . . It should be noted that the education of the indigenous population is carried out by the Catholic Missions, in conformity with an agreement signed twenty years ago between Portugal and the Holy See. According to this agreement, the Catholic Missions "are obliged to teach the Portuguese language exclusively in schools . . . [and] instruction must pursue objectives set forth in the Portuguese Constitution."
>
> . . . Allow me to quote a passage from a recent article from the

Cardinal Archbishop of Lourenço Marques, which appeared in the Magazine, *Portugal in Africa*, May-June 1960. The article reads: "What the missionaries hope to accomplish by the education and instruction of the native youth is to have the Church of Mozambique continue to remain at the side of Portugal." And again, "The missionary action brings honour to Portugal in the high international organizations and constitutes a solid support for Portuguese sovereignty...." This, my friends, is the civilizing and Christian mission carried out by Portugal. You be the judges.

In essence, the ideological approach of the rising African elite is to repudiate scathingly Christianity's association with colonialism. Whether or not, in the long run, this will impede personal commitment to Christian affiliation is impossible to predict. At present, thinking is dominated by an extreme and befuddled skepticism about the mission of Christianity in Africa.

The Psychological Legacy of Christianity

The claim is often made in elite circles that the very acceptance of Christianity by Africans constituted a form of cultural and psychological alienation. Christianity was presented, not simply as a religious doctrine, but as a sociocultural set of values and norms, which was deemed to be superior to anything offered by African culture. It is not surprising that a rise in self-consciousness among African intellectuals should cause many of them to react with hostility.

In a discussion of this with an African scholar, I was told: "In reality, too many Christians have shown us a cultural arrogance as shortsighted as the Western doctrine of racial superiority. In many instances, Christian institutions were called upon to support both racial supremacy and cultural imperialism. In Christian theology, God was presented as white, and all virtues, including aesthetic standards, were white. The psychological damage which this has done to the

Negro in the New World is well known to us. However, what is interesting is that Negro intellectuals in the New World have not reacted as sharply to this situation as has happened in Africa. Instead, doctrines which seek to counteract this psychological scar among Western Negroes have found currency only among the lower classes, like the Garvey movement, or the Black Muslim movement. In Africa, with the exception of the lower-class "Separatist and Independent churches,' the reverse is true."

Chief Awolowo, in his autobiography, confesses that as a boy he thought of the white man "as a superman," whose color "symbolized delicacy, innocence, and purity. . . . What a mighty man I thought he was, so especially favoured by God to have a white skin and to occupy such a position of exalted superiority."

The African intellectual's reaction to this process of self-alienation propels him toward a view similar to that of lower-class black nationalism in the United States. There are denials that this goes all the way over to black supremacy, but sometimes this distinction is not easy to defend. At the very least it is seeing things, including God, through the eyes of black men. It finds expression in African literature, as when the late R. G. Armattoe wrote:

> Our God is black
> Black of eternal blackness
> With large voluptuous lips
> Matted hair and brown liquid eyes;
> Figure of gainly form is He
> For in His image are we made
> Our God is black.

In "Negro Heaven" the same author wrote:

> And angels black as Indian ink
> And dark saints blacker still did sing.

This is more than an attempt to Africanize Christianity. It is a way of seeing the whole world through the black man's eyes. Melvin J. Lasky, an Englishman, has tried his hand at interpretation: "*What colour is God?* If European Christianity arrived to persuade Africans that He was white, African nationalism emerged to convince them that He was really black. This is a most natural transvaluation of colour values, and I find in Sundkler's study of Bantu prophets descriptions of what a heavenly apartheid would be: on those pearly gates was a sign which read FOR BLACK MEN ONLY. . . . African liberalism begins under the spell of the principle of whiteness, but African militancy triumphs with its reversal."

These "transvaluations" have permeated the political life of African nationalist leaders. Thomas Hodgkins, in his *Nationalism in Colonial Africa,* recalls that even in Ghana, with its comparatively high level of economic and educational development, the effort of the Convention People's Party to create a mass political movement involved the use of familiar religious rituals: the singing of "Lead, Kindly Light," the reciting of nationalist prayers, and a Creed in which Kwame Nkrumah took the place of Christ, while Sir Arden Clarke (then Governor of Ghana) played the role of Pontius Pilate. A similar phenomenon was reported in connection with Kikuyu nationalism in Kenya, where Jomo Kenyatta was identified in hymns with Jesus Christ. More recently, an editorial in the *Accra Evening News* exulted that "Nkrumahism is the highest form of Christianity," and solemnly informed readers that "the infant Christ sought refuge in Africa, and when Christ was being led to Golgotha it was an African volunteer who helped him bear the heavy burden."

The editorial continued: "Christian civilization is today busily dragging Christ to Golgotha [atomic tests in the Sahara], and an African again is bearing the cross for the son of man. This African is Kwame Nkrumah. Ye men of little faith, Pharisees, false prophets and friends, behold he comes disguised. But for Africa and the world, he may well be the second Christ [!] who cometh when the babes in the womb are suffering from Strontium 90. . . ."

These are some of the chaotic strands to be found at the fringes of cultural revivalism in Africa. How they might lead to some sort of distinctively African religious revivalism is far from clear. The elite community is in a repudiating mood as far as religion is concerned—and not yet in a constructive mood. Cultural revivalism is heavily sloganistic—"*la negritude*" and "African personality"—but there is no positive agreement on the content of a "revived" culture. What exists is an agreement in principle that a distinctively African identity is wanted, yet not without its borrowings from the best in the world's political, economic, cultural, and religious life.

The emotional conflicts and confusions that result from this effort to maintain cultural identity, and at the same time borrow the best from the civilizations of others, are captured by Can Themba in his *Requiem for Sophiatown:*

> I'll tell you. In the world today are poised against each other two massive ideologies: of the East and of the West. Both of them play international politics as if we're bound to choose between them. Between them only. We have just discovered that we can choose as we like, if we grow strong in our own character. But there is more to this. The West has had a damned long time to win us. Win us over to Western thinking. Western Christian way of living. Their ideas of democracy and their Christian values were wonderful, but they did not mean them.
>
> Let me explain. We are quite a religious people. We accept the idealism of Christianity. But in a stubborn, practical sense we believe in reality. Christian brotherhood must be real. Democracy must actually be the rule of the people: not of a white hobo over a black Master of Arts.
>
> To us, if a witch doctor says he'll bring rain, we do not only want to see the rain fall, but also the crops sprout from the earth.

That's what a rainmaker's for, nay? . . . So if the priest says God's on my side, I'd like to see a few more chances and a little less white-man's curses.

But in any case, Christianity is now an anemic religion. It cannot rouse the ancient in me—especially the Chak instinct I still have. Now, you and I are educated guys. We don't go for the witchcraft stuff. And we don't want to go for the jukebox stuff. But much as we deny it, we still want the thrill of the wild blood of our forefathers. The whites call it savagery. Ineradicable barbarism. But in different degrees we want the color and vibrant appeal of it all.

Cultural revivalism pulls the young African intellectual one way; Christian "idealism" and prestige pull him another. There is far more personal emotion involved than can be expressed in an outsider's calm survey.

Peter Abrahams, the West Indian writer, reports an incident in London back in the days when dreams of African independence were still the wild fancies of a few students: "The Circle [a secret political society] was proposed by Nkrumah and he asked that each of us spill a few drops of our own blood into a bowl and so take a blood oath of secrecy and dedication to the emancipation of Africa. Johnstone Kenyatta laughed at the idea; he scoffed at it as childish ju-ju. He conceived our struggle in modern, twentieth-century terms with no ritualistic nonsense. In the end, Francis Nkrumah drifted away from us and started his own little West African group. . . ."

Yet, the pages of Kenyatta's book *Facing Mount Kenya,* lay bare his own raw need to be part of the Kikuyu spiritual heritage. He dedicated the book to "Moigoi and Wamboi and all the dispossessed youth of Africa: for perpetuation and communion with ancestral spirits through the fight for African Freedom, and in the firm faith that the dead, the living and the unborn will unite to rebuild the destroyed shrines."

The basic problem of a member of the African elite is to think through his religious views in terms that match his experience. Older leaders, such as Kenyatta and Nkrumah, have minds which turn naturally to religious matters. In their earliest years they were strongly attracted to Christian teaching, but they soon found the various European forms of Christianity too pale and restricted for their emotional needs. Whatever Christianity was to mean to them, it would be "undenominational" in manifestation. Even so, it could never be enough to warm the ancient blood running through their veins. Both have sought a synthesis of the old ways with modern needs. Kenyatta spelled it out in *Facing Mount Kenya.* When Nkrumah returned to Ghana after his long exile as a student, his passion for "African ideals" was quickly inflated by popular rumor. Peter Abrahams writes: "Tribal myths grew up around him. He could make himself invisible at will. He could go without food and sleep and drink longer than ordinary mortals. He was, in fact, the reincarnation of some of the most powerful ancestral spirits."

In recent years, though their situations differed greatly, both Kenyatta and Nkrumah have continued to search for religious insights to match their experience. While in his Kenya prison, Kenyatta acquired a large collection of books on comparative religion, and he made a serious study of Oriental faiths. He says that he was particularly impressed with the *Bhagavad Gita.* Nkrumah, meanwhile, has read widely on Hinduism, Buddhism, Confucianism, and Islam. He has a sophisticated interest in theological problems and in the religious origins of philosophies of non-violence. When I talked with him in his presidential office in Accra, he picked up a battered brief case and drew out of it a prayer he said he had recently written for his morning meditations. Orthodox churchmen in Ghana think of Nkrumah as being cynically detached from their faith, and it is true that the prayer he showed me was not phrased in conventional Christian form, but it was anything but cynical and detached. He had obviously typed it himself, and then revised it many times by hand. It was warm, personal, and devout in tone. It was addressed to the "Eternal God of all men." But instead of closing with the customary Christian formula, it ended with a series of traditional African benedictions and blessings.

The attempt to forge a spiritual anchor for nationalist politics both challenges and bedevils the African elitist. Kenyatta and Nkrumah, with their natural philosophical bent, appreciate "undenominational" Christian idealism, but they have no desire for alignment with any of the competing forms of Christianity. Both are committed to cultural revivalism, which means an ardent interest in traditional African molds. Their wide-ranging minds are attracted to exploration of the world's great religions.

Another odyssey among the older leaders is that of Chief Awolowo, whose recent autobiography, *Awo: The Autobiography of Chief Obafemi Awolowo*, provides many insights into his particular kind of pilgrimage.

Awolowo's father was one of the first to embrace Christianity after missionaries came to Ikenne in 1896. The father brought not only his brothers into the Christian fold, but many outside the family circle as well. Awolowo describes him as "a conscientious Christian and an unfailing churchgoer," who "abhorred paganism, together with its innumerable rites, rituals and festivals. He impressed it upon me to shun anything connected with paganism. He had contempt for medicine-men and he openly pooh-poohed belief in witchcraft and wizardry."

Awolowo looks back on missionary activity in those early years with profound admiration. He refers to missionaries as "intrepid pioneers" who "reflected the spirit and teachings of Christ as much as any human being could, in their day-to-day contact with their new flock." He recalls being made to realize quite early in life that "Christianity was, of a surety, superior in many respects to paganism."

The mission provided Awolowo with an education, and he became an avid reader. "In the course of my incursion into the wide realm of literature, I came across a big tome of a book which was a collection of the essays and lectures of Robert G. Ingersoll." Awolowo was utterly fascinated. He found himself "racing breathlessly along with this amazing man," and by the time he had finished his literary excursion with Ingersoll, he had become "a hearty admirer of agnosticism." He plunged into other heretical works: Tom Paine, T. H. Huxley, and the like. "From the time of my mental acquaintance and communion with Ingersoll, I attended church occasionally, when there was a wedding ceremony, memorial service, or when my wife successfully insisted on my keeping her company. I found it hard to disbelieve in or to doubt the existence of God. But I vehemently disavowed the legends and fictions which the Israelites and their successors in dogma have woven around Him. I positively held the view that, down the ages, different groups of men have at different times created their own God in their own warped image, and that so long as these dogmatic erring fanatics continued to project their own self-created God instead of the true God, so long would there be room for rational men with the courage of their conviction to feel impelled to repudiate the man-made God."

From 1944 to 1946, Awolowo was in England, where he "did not cross the portals of a church except for sight-seeing to Westminster Abbey and St. Paul's Cathedral." He did, however, attend some of the Sunday meetings of the South Place Ethical Society at Conway Hall. "Each time I attended the meeting," he recalls, "I always came away with the question in my mind: 'Why this imperfect and irrational imitation of the Christian mode of worship?' It dawned upon me, more than ever before, that human beings naturally love rituals and ceremonies. Whether they believe in God or not, they always like to worship and venerate something: a flag or a shrine; the tomb or effigy of a dead hero or a person or presence of a living one. . . . I sincerely thought that something was missing at the Conway Hall meetings . . . and a process of re-evaluation of Christian ideals and practices as compared with agnostic, rationalistic or atheistic concepts was generated within me. *Eventually I returned to the Holy Bible and to the Christian fold.* [italics mine] Throughout the period of oscillation between agnosticism and Christianity, my wife stood immovably for the latter. Her constant admonitions and steadfastness did more than anything else to restrain me from going beyond the point of no return."

Awolowo's journey is significantly different from Nkrumah's or Kenyatta's. He has brought his personal Christian commitment into adjustment with his experience and nationalist politics, but not without this sober warning: "It is my candid view. . . that the vast majority of Christians, including the clergy, are too ill-equipped dialectically to combat with success the aggressive detractors and traducers of our great religion."

A gaping pitfall in the path of younger elitists who might follow Awolowo's lead is a generalized suspicion that Christian spokesmen are not only "ill-equipped dialectically," but are also incapable of transcending a Western bias. An incident following in the wake of the Congo's troubles illustrates this extreme sensitivity and suspiciousness. A group of Congolese teen-age boys was brought to the United States to participate in a special Y.M.C.A. program in the summer of 1961. Their experience brought this seething "Open Letter to the Young Men's Christian Association of Pittsburgh:"

The Congolese Student Union of the United States of America was highly disappointed with the goals of your policy concerning the Republic of the Congo through her young citizens.

The statements made by Mr. Edwin M. Bodenbaugh (The *New York Times,* July 1, 1961, p. 3), a Pittsburgh industrialist and Director of the Y.M.C.A. demonstrates clearly your narrow, selfish and colonialist attitude toward the Congo whose sons you have invited to this country primarily for political and ideological indoctrination.

According to the industrialist named above, "Previous trips involved college students whose ideas are already molded; high school students are less likely to have fixed political ideas."

The Director of the Y.M.C.A. of Pittsburgh, for the sake of American Democracy, goes on to say that "as a result of the trip the Congolese boys will be exposed to American democratic ideals." What a shame and indignation for us to realize that the hospitality of this "Young Men's Christian Association" is not conditioned by Christian Charity but politically. *This is what justifies the suspicions of Africans over the Christian enterprise in Africa* [italics mine].

The Congolese Students Union of the United States of America is aware of the maneuvers affecting the Congo's instability. So far as the policy of your Christian Association is directed toward humiliation of the Republic of the Congo by maintaining or gaining ideological control over her sons' minds, we advise you to send back these young boys to our homeland. . . .

Anyone who inquires these days into the religious mood of Africa's young intellectual class finds this burr of suspicion riding close to the surface of the skin. As near as a non-African can get to understanding the psychological Christian heritage of Africa's elite is to appreciate the intensity with which the idea of being "black European Christians" is rejected. By no means should this be oversimplified as a rejection of Christianity. It does not mean this at all—at least not yet. The African elite is in the midst of a cultural encounter which generates suspicion, sensitivity, and a demand for self-knowledge before any additional spiritual commitments are made.

The Moral Basis of "New" African Societies

In many ways this is an awkward subject. There exists as yet no large body of coherent thought among African intellectuals as to the essence of a "Good" which might transcend the prejudices of individuals or groups. But J. B. Danquah, the Ghanaian logician, made a systematic attempt to mine what is truly *African* (at least in a geographical sense) in moral philosophy. In his classic, *The Akan Doctrine of God*, he has sought to identify principles of morality in traditional African society. The notion of the "Good" in African life is derived, he says, from the African's knowledge of God as the Great Ancestor. "He is," Danquah writes, "a true high God and manlike ancestor of the first man. As such ancestor He deserves to be worshipped, and is worshipped in the visible ancestral head, the good chief of the community (of whatever size). All ancestors who are honored as such are in the line of the Great Ancestor. Every head of a community, because he is in such a line, must live according to the dignity of the first. To fall below that dignity is a falling below the dignity of God. The elder or head of the family is the nearest of such ancestors."

Danquah explains that the head of an Akan family is called Nana, just as God, the first ancestor, is called Nana. The chief of the tribe, race, or nation is called Nana, because he too is in the footsteps of the Great Ancestor. All are worshipful, even as the Great Ancestor is worshipful. How does this extrude a moral philosophy? Danquah answers: "The Great Ancestor is the great father, and all men of the blood of that ancestor are of Him, and are of one blood with all other men created of His blood and breath. Life, human life, is one continuous blood, from the originating blood of the Great Source of that blood. The continuance of that blood in the continuance of the community is the greatest single factor of existence. It is an idea worshipful in itself, and the purpose of *community* is that the value of that life should be continuously kept abreast of the dignity of the ancestor. Anything short of that ideal makes life a degradation, a contradiction of what men of the ancestral blood, one in the Great Ancestor, should be inspired by."

Danquah claims for the Akan apprehension of God a direct moral consequence, or rather, a series of interlocking moral consequences which he calls ethical canons. These canons, in Danquah's view, are not merely "traditional." They can be "related to current modes of thought on the value of man's place as a living organism in the social universe." In brief, they can provide a moral base for "new" African societies.

The first canon declares that every effort at goodness is conserved as merit in the soul and aids the progressive fulfilment by the individual of his destiny. Danquah says: "Our mastery or dominance of the natural order, or of physical nature . . . registers for us our first victory for the spiritual. The traditional or the scientific knowledge, which the growing community acquires or possesses over the processes of nature, is therefore destined to be used by the community for the furtherance of its own good in order that men of the community should live well."

What is clear, says Danquah, is that "the cumulative experience of the community, its experience or effort in goodness, its knowledge of the laws of life, its struggle against disease and ignorance, its effort to eliminate pain, nay, even its ordering of human relations by the laws of society—are all modes of traditional inheritance which make for a greater and a more constant achievement and a greater and more real correlation of total effort of virtuous men with the complete good."

The second canon affirms that moral progress is "constant and continuous in proportion as individual gains or merits of the past are handed on as tradition to form the basis of racial experience." Here Danquah stresses the positive role of tradition in African life; the ability not only to hand on accumulated knowledge and virtue, but also to pass along wisdom about resistances to progress.

The third canon establishes principles of leadership and puts a moral foundation under education: "Racial progress facilitates the development of innate characteristics in outstanding individuals who consciously liberate such characteristics to strengthen the inherited tradition."

Thus, as Danquah expresses it: ". . . the surest way to goodness and to God is education." As for the "outstanding individuals"—the great warriors, statesmen, religious leaders, thinkers, etc.—they are the bridges who make it possible for the high ideals to pass "from the family to the tribe or race, to the clan or nation, and finally to humanity as such—to a recognition of the one true family of man, humanity itself, as the only complete and justifiable objective, the only 'family' for the total good of God." This comprises:

The fourth canon—"The conscious liberation of outstanding characteristics which demand corresponding fields for expansion leads to the comprehension of greater social wholes and the logical recognition of humanity as the all-embracing ideal for fulfilling and developing racial experience."

There is no higher wisdom than the knowledge that life's meanings, values, and harmonies are richer, the more broadly they are shared. A united status for all mankind is the greatest of revelations, the most glorious of ideals. Yet, because of "man's own obstreperous intransigence," it is difficult to predict how this moral advance is to shape itself. The possibilities for future advance are indicated, however, in:

The fifth canon—"Absolute experience, or realization of the whole, remains unattainable so long as racial experience excludes part of the whole, and the moral might of mankind falls short of the absolute thing."

The stubborn obduracy of the human species makes any easy optimism senseless, yet life "would seem to carry man along in its current, despite the resistance his selfish will offers against his own good." Man goes out of his way to place obstacles in his own path, he "sets up meaningless systems and authorities, he idolizes senseless group distinctions, he invents powers and machines of destruction, and generates and accommodates large masses of physical and moral evil. . . ." Still, progress is made and "the hope for the attainment of the whole is more than an ideal hope . . . it is the destiny of man."

Danquah argues that the Akan moral canons ought to squelch once and for all the notion that non-European races are incapable of any originality which is not merely "primitive." The working tools of Akan moral and religious practices, while distinctive of Akan thought, demonstrate that African traditional concepts are "readily reducible to terms already established in the accepted body of human knowledge." Africans, in other words, have within their own culture the makings of a moral base for "new" African societies. He claims that these ideas are neither pro- nor anti-Christian. In a poem written during his student days he sketches the pertinent theological conclusions:

The All of God is God.
God is not Christian,
Nor Moslem,
Nor King,
Nor Three,

Nor One,
Nor Many,
But all.
All is all all.
All is common.
All all is God.
God is common.

It would be a wild exaggeration to claim that African elite sentiment clusters in any substantial way around Danquah's work, but elitists frequently refer to it, and it is an important point of reference in their answers to queries about how African intellectuals propose to undergird their rising societies with a moral consensus.

Others are also trying their hand, using the "political" framework which most of the African elite prefer these days to theology. Léopold Senghor conceives of the "Negro African Nation" as a type of African socialist community, or "communal society," or better, "a communion of souls." For him, *people* and *community* are interchangeable terms. The ideal of the new society is a community "where each individual will identify himself with the collectivity and vice versa. But the *unanimity,* the *communion of souls,* is not enough. For the people to become a nation, the individual must grow. . . . We must assure a cultural basis for the future Nation, by defining the essential characteristics of traditional Negro African civilization which, blending with European . . . contributions, will undergo a renaissance."

In his essay called "African Socialism," Senghor points an accusing finger at Soviet Communism: "The anxiety for human dignity, the need for freedom—man's freedoms, the freedoms of collectivities—which animate Marx's thought and provide its revolutionary ferment—this anxiety and this need are unknown to communism. . . . The 'dictatorship of the proletariat,' which was to be only temporary, becomes the dictatorship of the party and state by perpetuating itself. 'The Soviet Union,' said Mamadou Dia [a Senegalese] on his return from Moscow, 'has succeeded in building socialism but at the sacrifice of religion, of the soul.' "

But Senghor also has harsh words for the "capitalist construction in the United States of America, the American way of life, with high salaries, frigidaires, washing machines and television sets." He predicts that the new African societies "shall not be won over by the regime of liberal capitalism and free enterprise. We cannot close our eyes to segregation, although the Federal Government combats it; nor can we accept the *elevation of material success to a way of life* [italics mine]."

African socialism, he says, stands for "a middle course." It is a revolutionary thrust which intends to integrate moral and religious values with political and economic ones. In this revolution the Negro African must play a crucial role; he must bring his unique contribution to the construction of a new planetary civilization. Then Senghor concludes:

> *Man* remains our first consideration: he constitutes our *measure*. That is what the man represents on the flag of Mali, with his roots in the soil, and his eyes turned heavenward. I shall end by paraphrasing Dostoevski, the Russian. A nation that refuses to keep its rendezvous with history, that does not believe itself to be the bearer of a unique message—that nation is finished, ready to be placed in a museum. The Negro African is not finished even before he gets started. Let him speak; above all let him act. Let him bring, like a leaven, his message to the world in order to build a universal civilization.

Léopold Senghor is a Roman Catholic. The country of which he is president, Senegal, is predominantly Moslem. He takes pride in this fact. In 1960, when he withdrew Senegal from the Mali Federation, and was not immediately recognized by the United States, he chided the Eisenhower administration, saying that Senegal was more democratic than the United States in at least one respect: His religion was not held against him in Senegal as Mr. Kennedy's apparently was in the United States. American voters proved Senghor wrong, but the debate over the issue impressed him.

It is worth noting that Senghor's vision of the New African Society is moralistic and "spiritual," but not discernibly "Christian." In many of Africa's leaders there are strong strains of the eighteenth-century's "enlightenment" and the twentieth-century's humanism. When "Zikhism" was riding the crest of Nigeria's struggle for independence, its elements were analyzed by the Nigerian author, Orizu. He concluded that Dr. Azikiwe was a humanist, whose spiritual fonts were Jefferson and Tom Paine. Dr. Azikiwe's speech at his inauguration as the first African Governor General of Nigeria was a peroration, significantly enough, on "Expansion of the Stature of Man."

I was present at the gaudy Palais de la Nation in Leopoldville, when the ill-fated Patrice Lumumba assumed office as Prime Minister of the Congo, and promised: "We are going to put an end to the suppression of free thought and make it possible for all citizens fully to enjoy the fundamental liberties set down in the declaration of the Rights of Man. We are going to succeed in suppressing all discrimination—no matter what it may be—and give each individual the just place to which his human dignity, his work, and his devotion to his country entitle him."

Later I had a conversation with the slender, bearded Mr. Lumumba. He seemed even younger than his thirty-four years as he described his disenchantment with the Roman Catholic faith in which he had been raised. He was, as he put it, "content to be a secularist." He felt that the Church was incapable of understanding the "humanistic society" African nationalists would build.

Sékou Touré, the forty-year-old president of Guinea, and a nominal Moslem, is another of the leaders who speaks with a humanistic tongue. When he addressed the General Assembly of the United Nations in 1959, he said:

> The practical difficulties of life have taught the African virtues which are daily exercised by the most humble of these men. These are the virtues of solidarity, love of justice, faith in man, the sense of brotherhood, and respect for society. Africa intends to cultivate and foster these virtues and to bring them to the world as a first token of its participation in universal life. . . . I sincerely believe that this period of history will witness the beginning of a new phase in the development of humanity, one which will continue, without overturning either the present structure of the world or the system of values of nations and peoples. I sincerely believe that the final destiny of nations will depend principally upon the nature of their involvement and the extent of the responsibilities which they will take in the building of the universal society, as well as in the building of a new world. . . . I appeal to nations . . . to all the peoples ready to participate in the building of a new world, the world of the victory of intelligence and of human values.

It is to be hoped that Dr. Danquah was aware of Touré's use of the *fourth canon* of Akan morality in this speech to the world body.

Thomas Diop of Senegal, at an International Conference on "Representative Government and National Progress," held at the University College, Ibadan, under the auspices of The Congress of Cultural Freedom, outlined what he considered to be the moral components of "African personality" around which the new societies would be built. He listed:

1. An inflexible will to be freely and fully itself in all fields.
2. A firm will to restore African cultural values to their rightful place.
3. The determination to enrich its own civilization by intro-

ducing into it those features of other civilizations which seem to it worthy of contributing to the creation of a universal civilization.

4. An extraordinary adaptability that is evident throughout the history of Africa.
5. A very acute sense of justice in human relations.
6. A great and honest spirit of brotherly solidarity extending to all the peoples of the earth.
7. A proud determination to contribute fully to world interchange.

Diop then further emphasized the last two moral components of "African personality" with this editorial comment: ". . . the African's spirit of solidarity is not limited to the sons of Africa. It extends to all peoples, since these peoples also belong to the great human family which we must serve in the interest of all."

Danquah, Senghor, Azikiwe, Lumumba, Touré, and Diop, though they speak with varied accents, bear down hard on the theme of solidarity, communion, community. In this they are uniformly faithful to the traditional African spiritual belief that society is more than "an aggregate of individuals." Whether through nostalgia or realism, their aspirations for modern political morality are supported by a faith that the traditional systems of social relations were able to harmonize the strivings of individuals with the requirements of group life. Their concern now is to find a similar balance between the needs of a modern state and strong individual self-expression. Yet none is provincial in his nationalism. All are attracted powerfully by universalism, without regard to race, color, or religion.

Striking also is their self-evident optimism about man and his destiny in the world. Whatever Christianity's other influences on elite thought, it has not succeeded in "convicting" African intellectuals of original sin. They are faithful to

Nommo, man's power over the word. They are convinced of the ultimate victory of intelligence and human values. Danquah describes the traditional Akan belief in reincarnation as faith in the ultimate virtuous destiny of the soul. The soul returns to earth, "imperfect, certainly, or he would not need to return, but not complete." Few intellectuals would admit to a belief in reincarnation, but they hold fast to faith in the destined triumph of a fully mature and integrated humanity.

The impression grows that whatever their private theological beliefs, members of the African elite visualize the moral base of both their traditional and emerging societies as man-centered or humanistic. When they appeal to "traditional African spiritual values" they have in mind no pantheon of gods and spirits, but idealized memories of what one of my African friends describes as "the good old days when face to face contact was possible; when the bonds of the family were sufficiently strong to provide limitless personal security even without bank accounts, when Freud and Jung could not have found employment, in communities where neither Adam Smith nor Karl Marx could have won a debate, though both would have been listened to and told where each was wrong!"

The moral foundation of "new" African societies is seen by the African elite as being anchored in the best of traditional values: shared feelings about the primacy of human life in a community or "communion of souls"; an "acute sense of justice in human relations"; and the "great and honest spirit of brotherly solidarity."

Moral and Religious Training in African Education

The next few years should produce a flood of advice from African intellectuals on this issue. As I write, there is little organized guidance from African sources. The present need for education *of any kind* is so urgent that it supersedes all other considerations; but there are stirrings of future "great debates" on the spiritual philosophy of African education.

As the handmaiden of religion, the mission school has traditionally taught the creeds and precepts of Christianity according to the lights of the various sponsoring denominations and sects. During the period of colonialism, denominational Christianity was the substance of religious education in virtually all elementary, secondary and university-level schools. This pattern is likely to persist wherever churches are encouraged or permitted to operate an educational system. In heavily Moslem areas it goes without saying that Islam is the basis of moral training in most schools.

There is a push throughout the independent areas for state-run educational systems. There is little doubt that the question of religious instruction in public schools will become a controversial issue. The government of Ghana, when it took over University College, promptly knocked theological education out of the curriculum. Because of strong feelings about "decolonializing" education by stressing "African values," it is likely that a powerful segment of intellectual opinion will favor removing religious instruction from schools. This is compatible with the prevailing view that organized religious bodies should be kept separate from the state.

I have recorded some conversations on this subject with African university students. Their comments are of value chiefly for their emotional content. No one, certainly, would be impressed by their logic; but such emotions are the seedbeds of future controversies.

"For the life of me," said one of these students, "I would not allow my child to suffer from the religious mentality which befuddled my thinking and vision for so long. When I look back at my past, and that of my family, I think that the chief result of our Christian training was to make us incredibly naïve. All you have to do is go to England or America and you will find out that they really don't pay any attention to religion. See where they are today! If we are to make any progress, religion must be thrown out of every school in the country. Don't think that I am harsh, or that I am not grateful for the education I received from the missionaries. But as far as the religious side of it is concerned, it was a no-good education."

Another student complained that religious training in school was a threat rather than an aid to morality. "You don't teach morality in school," he said. "That is something taught at home. I think Africans have a sound idea about moral training. Let the schools teach math, science, and the arts. Leave it to the parents to teach morality. They know what is good for their children better than any teacher. How would you like a beatnik teacher teaching moral principles to your children? Imagine all these psychological crazes these days! Is that what you want? Some smart aleck telling your children that there is nothing sacred about sex? This stuff on undisciplined self-expression? No! No! No! Morality is what you acquire in your family and in your community. You watch the lives of the adults and follow their example. It's up to the adults in the community to show good example and the children will follow suit."

If exasperated protest is the theme of some young intellectuals when they think about the "spiritual" side of education, there are others with steadier and more sober reflections. An African political scientist told me: "My own feeling is that we're bound to get a whole array of personality distortions. There's too much change all at once. These processes have just begun to take place and will be intensified in the years ahead. They are not the kinds of problems society can legislate, nor can they be checked by appeals to this or that religious system imposed on the schools. I do not believe that the moral life of any people can be fostered by including creeds and theological maxims in the school curriculum. On the other hand, there is room for the propagation of such moral values as a given community, by experience and judgment, believes to be worthwhile for the happiness of its members. Such values should be fostered in the schools. However, what is needed in African schools is the kind of training which enables the individual to establish an identity with his community, with his culture, and with the collective excellences of mankind. I share the views of those who believe that the development of discipline and character are essential parts of education. However, any system of moral training of the African, embodied in education, is only a partial answer to the problems of life. I think that the African can discover his standards of morality, his aesthetic values, and even his religion, only when he has become involved in the fate and destiny of his people, only when he can share the joys and miseries of those around him, and only when he can fully participate in the collective experience of the larger humanity. The big question for me is how the elite can be educated so as not to lose their identity as Africans. We've got to learn how to build new societies in which traditional values are utilized. This is the crucial spiritual problem for African education. We talk about it a lot, but all we've got so far is agreement that we need a solution."

There is a flamboyant kind of unity among the elite as to the essential tasks of independent African governments. There is no such unity when it comes to spelling out forms of moral and spiritual training in education. The sharp-tongued Ayo Ogunshaye, who has little patience with mystiques of "African personality," was asked for his prescription. He wrote: "Oh, I suppose it would go something like this: Be yourselves. Know your past and your culture, for a people without a sense of values and the past is like a ship without a rudder.

To your cultural heritage don't hesitate to add from other cultures some ideas and some techniques which you think will help you build a better world. In doing this you will only be returning the compliment of the Western World, which did not hesitate to draw on your art and music in order to revitalize its own. In the world of culture we are all builders, all borrowers and lenders."

The moral basis of education in Africa is yet to emerge as what Herbert Passin calls "a product of an intricate dialectics between the ideas of its elites and the changing realities with which they are called upon to deal."

Is Communism a Spiritual Alternative?

Suddenly Communism in Africa is a major international issue. No more than five years ago it would have been completely unnecessary to mention it in this book. Now the Soviet bloc and mainland China have succeeded in gaining important footholds in Africa. Their cultural envoys, trade missions, and technicians move about briskly. There are local pro-Communists, and small but ardent African Communist groups. It would be blind to ignore Communism's challenge in Africa, but in our part of the world we tend to err at the opposite extreme. The best "political" treatment of this problem, in my opinion, is Walter Z. Laquer's article in the July, 1961, issue of *Foreign Affairs.* The question with which this book is concerned is the strength or weakness of Communism's spiritual appeal to the African elite.

Peter Ritner, in *The Death of Africa,* claimed that Africa's *denouement* was certain unless there was immediate outside aid. Africa cannot possibly save herself, Ritner argued, yet she can be saved, and he pled for massive American assistance. African elite reaction to Ritner's thesis has been interesting. The elite resent both his diagnosis and his cure.

Ritner is accused of following the old "white man's burden" line, and of suggesting that the fruits of capitalism are Africa's only alternative to a disastrous slide into Communism. Ritner would have a right to feel aggrieved at both allegations. If there is any comfort for the West in this stormy response to efforts such as Ritner's, it must be found in the irritable denial by most of the elite that Africa *must choose* between Communism and the West.

President Nkrumah has frequently trumpeted: "Africa faces neither East nor West, but forward!" This slogan is applicable to more than political or military alignments. It symbolizes the full terrain of self-conscious African development. It points to matters of the spirit.

The consensus among intellectuals is that Communism has little spiritual appeal for Africans. Sékou Touré, considered by many in the West to be the African ruler most susceptible to Eastern bloc influence, has frequently and emphatically rejected Communism as an African way of life: "I refuse to allow the P.D.G. [his party] to follow the ideological line of communism. If certain people wish to do so, let them found a Guinea Communist Party, but they must realize that the P.D.G. will oppose them under my leadership. Communism is not the way for Africa. The class struggle here is impossible, for there are no classes, but only social strata. The fundamental basis of our society is the family and the village community."

When asked if his country was modeling itself after China, Touré replied: "Why should we? I have just been over China. It is a very different country from ours. I found nothing in China's experience that could interest us."

While gathering material for his book, *Profiles of African Leaders,* Thomas Melady visited a bookshop in Guinea's capital city of Conakry, which had a reputation for featuring Communist literature. There he found a good many youthful

Guineans browsing. When Melady left the store, he was followed by a young man who obviously wanted to talk. Melady invited him to a coffee house, and after a friendly conversation, the Guinean said: "Don't worry too much about the Communist bookstore. The Communists have made one big mistake. A great number of their books abuse God and say nasty things about him. We Africans just naturally believe in a Supreme Being—we believe in some kind of God, perhaps the Christian God, the Moslem Allah, or it may be the God in the mountains, but we believe in God and there are few of us who could ever embrace, philosophically speaking, Marxist communism."

Nbabaningi Sithole offers confirmation, but in a different vein:

> So far as we have examined our topic [Africa and Communism], we find no relation between African nationalism and Russian communism. African nationalism springs from inside Africa, and not from Moscow. If the African can continue to hate communism with all his heart, and soul, and might, just as he does European imperialism, so much to the good, because to prefer one brand of imperialism to another is the very height of folly and a fatal miscalculation. Africa can derive no more and no less benefit from communism than from European imperialism. Her real welfare does not lie in preferring either one or the other, but in rejecting both, since under one or the other she will continue to occupy a secondary position and suffer indignities that go with such a position.

The weight of elite sentiment emphasizes the formidable barriers in the way of Communist penetration of the African soul. The newly free African countries are fiercely jealous of their independence. Pan-Africanists have already discovered that an awful lot of water is going to flow through the great river beds before any organic union of African states is realized. Communism inevitably clashes with nationalism both in its localized and Pan-African forms. It collides also with *la negritude*, African "socialism," and the whole African effort to evolve identity and an indigenous synthesis of politics, economics, culture and religion.

In addition to the barricades of nationalism and other expressions of African identity and solidarity, Communism runs afoul of the same tribal and tradition-centered resistances that plague the nationalist movements themselves. Communism, moreover, would have to make itself acceptable to the powerful family ties and kinship feelings which are the cement of African social life. A monumental challenge to Marxist-Leninist theoreticians!

Though I can hardly recommend them as cool, objective appraisals, I offer the statements of three quite typical members of the elite as characteristic reactions to Communism as a spiritual alternative for African souls.

Said one: "Do you think we are going to substitute Peiping and Moscow for Rome and Mecca? That's how to lose your identity. Colonialism and imperialism have taught us our most important lesson. No more brainwashing! No more supremacy, whether it's white or yellow."

The second declared: "From what I have heard of Communist countries, they sound drab to me. Maybe we suffered colonialism as long as we did because it didn't succeed in disturbing our rhythm. I don't mean to say that I approve of colonialism in any form. I consider colonialism an evil. The white man's evil. But Communism would want to suppress the rhythm, that vital force, in me. Colonialism tried to do the same thing. Christianity tried to do the same thing. Both failed. Communism is going to fail too. There is something deep in me which hates drabness, and Communism has too much of this bug. Without the vital force, the rhythm, the Chaka in me, how would I survive? How would the race survive? You answer those questions. Then tell me about

Communism. What we want is Afrocracy—the system that will permit my rational self to grow and intermix with my irrational being. These smart white people who know everything don't even know that rhythm is part of life too!"

A third put it this way: "You know what Nkrumah has done. He disbanded the Communists. Nasser did the same thing. Touré and Mboya say, neither China nor Russia can speak for us. This is a new day, it's Africa's day. It's not Russia's day. For that matter, it's not Washington's day either. Let Washington get rid of its own Ku Klux Klan and neo-colonialism. This is Africa. Our Africa!"

It would be dim-witted, however, to assume that the case is closed. Orthodox Communists are at present a mere handful in Africa, but they are as long on patience as they are on confidence in their ultimate success. Until recently they were content to march in step with nationalist leaders even when they were practicing Christians like Mboya and Nyerere, undenominational Christians like Nkrumah, and Moslems like Touré. African nationalism viewed the West as the main enemy of liberation, and nationalist leaders were helping, wittingly or unwittingly, to build a common anti-Western front.

Recently there has been a hardening of the Communist line. The well-known nationalist leaders are now lumped in African Communistic publications as "national bourgeoisie." They are pilloried as unfit guides of nationalist movements toward "true" socialism. In the January, 1961, issue of *The African Communist*, theoretician F. Kumalo defined the new tack: "They [the present nationalist leaders] are apt to be narrow, selfishly hidebound and conservative. They are apt to be guided not by the interests of the masses but by their own special, minority class interests. Often they are parochial, chauvinistic, and lacking broad vision. They are usually opportunistic, tend to compromise with the colonialists for small gains at the sacrifice of principle, because they fear the revolutionary activities of the masses of workers and rural people."

Another issue of the same publication broadened the attack on political leaders to include the entire African elite: "In conditions of modern society, the intellectuals occupy a middle position between the rulers and the ruled, the bourgeoisie and the proletariat.... Many of these intellectuals vacillate between one camp and another, are always swinging helplessly between the oppressors and the oppressed.... We must remember that it [the elite] as a group is inherently unstable and unfit for leadership."

What this means, of course, is that the elite cannot be trusted unless it joins the Communist movement. And the Communist movement, insignificantly small though it may be in Africa, is backed by a world-wide ideological apparatus which generates a tremendous spiritual impact on people frustratedly clawing their way out of humiliation and misery. Minor as Leninist influence is in present-day Africa, it goes on sowing seeds which marked failure on the part of current nationalist regimes could conceivably mature.

Part of our spiritual problem with respect to Africa is to deal discriminatingly with the anti-Western, often anti-Christian, and frequently quasi-Leninist slogans of the very same elite the orthodox Leninists attack. Add to this the apparent readiness of radical (though non-Communist) nationalist leaders in Africa to do business with Moscow, Prague, and Peiping as well as with Washington, Paris, and London, and you describe the awesome temptation we must somehow learn to resist: The temptation to yoke radical nationalists and Communists together as the enemies of God's faithful. The men who today drum the tunes in African life have no intention of permitting the Communist world to become the spiritual source of the music. They have identical feelings toward the West, but there is an important difference. The soul-scarring experiences have been with the West, with the Christian white man. There have been no similar experiences with Russians or with Communists. While there is no *positive* pull toward either West or East, there are stronger (and more personal) negative reactions toward the West.

The future of Communism as a form of spiritual commitment in Africa is still to unfold. Prevention of its spread includes the West's material aid for economic development, but something else is also needed. It is spiritual and intellectual collaboration given in a fraternal way among equals. This is a challenge the West has yet to prove it can fully meet.

In Search of a Self

I have said much about the "revival of African values" and the "march of nationalism." It is easy to assume that nothing more is involved here than a simple cause-and-effect relationship. African personality and African religions were overwhelmed by Western culture during the colonial period, and now, as the dominating weight of the West is lifted, the African spirit reasserts itself with the emotional support of nationalism. While this explanation has common-sense merit, in that it accounts logically for the surface situation, I am certain that it fails to come to terms with the deeper spiritual struggle of the African elite—that is, the search for a self.

Self-identity has become, in my opinion, the agonizingly serious problem of the African elite. It is a problem which bears strangely little relationship, at the moment, to whether a member of the elite describes himself as a Christian, a Moslem, an agnostic or a secularist.

The African intellectual is first of all an African. If he

could have remained in his traditional setting, and if his traditional setting had remained undisturbed, his self-identity would never have been a problem. His place in the world would be definite and precise. Even if he were moved to ask searching questions about life's mysteries, he would still be sustained by basic affirmations of who he was, what he was, and where he fitted into the scheme of things. His energies would have been mastered, trained, channeled, and coordinated with the general life of his family, clan, and tribe. He would stand, not as an individual, but as an organic link in life's chain of past members who are *teme,* present members who are visible, and future members who are to come into being.

The encounter between Africa and the West is a terribly complex matter, but one of its results is the creation of the new leader—the African with Westernized education, the man capable of interpreting the experiences of his people, not so much through the accumulated wisdom and values of African traditions as through the cultural, political, economic, and social values of the West.

In earlier days, Western-educated Africans became ardent converts to Western civilization, with its power and promise of salvation. They embraced Christianity, attacked the old customs and beliefs, and sang the praises of democracy and science. This is not to say that they repudiated their African heritage or allowed themselves to be used as front-men for missionaries or colonial administrators. To be sure, some of them were manipulated, and a few sold out; but most were sincerely devoted to the cause of reforming their overpowered and disintegrating African societies with the Western gospel of Christianity, democracy, and modernity. They were appalled at the gulf of power separating their people from the West. They hacked away at the tangle of old customs and traditions, not because they were senseless idol-smashers, but because they genuinely wished to tear the dead hand from the throat of their culture. The attraction of Christianity was cultural rather than theological. It was seen as a means of reconstructing rather than uprooting African personality.

The tragedy of Christian missionary work in Africa has been the failure to see this spiritual aspiration in its true light. For the most part, those Africans who supinely conformed to the mores of the mission compound were looked upon as the admirable converts, while abler and more energetic Africans—those determined to relate Christianity to African culture and history—were frequently condemned for "clinging to the pagan past."

It was these clingers "to the pagan past" who were to take up the great cause of political justice for their people; and here the missions, by and large, made a second monumental error: They did everything in their power to isolate the African mission enterprise from politics. Political activity was looked upon as a sin hardly less heinous than polygamy or female circumcision.

Many of the African elite began to find a new sense of value in their ancestral cultures. Kenyatta, when he was interviewed in 1948 at the Githunguri school of which he was headmaster, said: "You ask me what kind of line I am taking? Well, I think the best way to put it would be to say that I am cutting dead wood out of a lot of our old African beliefs, and I am reinforcing what I think are some of the best things in our African way of life. I am sending them out with something that I hope is going to work. I want them to be proud of being Africans! I don't want to make a lot of Black Englishmen!"

What began as enthusiasm for the Western gospel was

transformed into anti-Westernism. It became the "new" new gospel. The major evils of African life were laid at the doorstep of Western colonialism. The elite leaders, with their feet now marching to the drums of nationalism, rallied the masses behind them as "collective suffering servants" of imperialism, whose destiny was to bear to victory the gospel of Africanism, not only for the salvation of their African sons and grandsons, but also for the proper chastisement and redemption of the materialistic and warlike white man.

A period of struggle for independence is an epic period. Christians, Moslems, pagan chiefs, socialists, Communists, democrats, intellectuals, and illiterate villagers—all were united in the common effort. But the achievement of independence is in some ways like the end of a dream. It is one thing for prophets in the midst of an epic contest to conjure up visions of a New Jerusalem. It is quite another matter to deal with the internal, external, psychological, political, economic, social, and cultural pressures of a newly independent sovereign state.

In the independent areas, the role of the elite begins almost at once to change. In the march to freedom they were the creative minority, the new "priests," the molders and shapers and revivers of African culture. But once the walls of freedom have been scaled, the elite must become the technicians of the new order. They must accept their "assignments" to staff the government services, run the businesses, teach in the schools. The heady atmosphere of nationalist struggle becomes the stifling climate of making a hundred daily decisions, some of them incredibly petty and pedestrian.

"African personality," as a slogan and rallying cry, is a magnificent and moving ideal. But Africans are human beings, and the frailties of human flesh and spirit will out.

William Condon, the Gambian novelist, tells in his story,

The African, of the return to his homeland of a young West African, after several years of study in England:

> I came back to a stimulated land, pepped up into frantic, exhausting activity. It was not merely physical appearances that had altered so completely, the buildings, harbors, roads, bridges and so on, although change here was marvelous enough. Much more fascinating to me were the changes in the people and, I soon found, much more disturbing, too. New motives for action, new attitudes toward others, were . . . apparent. . . . There were new lusts too, which I did not remember being so blatantly indulged formerly—the lust for quick power, for quick riches; the unconcern as to what methods were employed in the process; the readiness to use, and even deliberately to foster, age-old tribal animosities. These had now been given a terribly sharp edge. . . . It was not that the African was just a nice chap, innocent and simple, who had been corrupted overnight by too intimate an association with an evil acquaintance. Rather . . . , we had reached a point where we were finding it increasingly difficult to keep a foothold on anything. We were in danger of losing our sense of direction, of purpose, of faith in ourselves.

It is a characteristic of the elite that its members have Condon's ability to look at themselves and their new nations with detachment. They are reasonably at home in the West, and they are certainly at home in Africa, but they are not completely comfortable in either place. Much that they know about African history, customs, traditions, and the like they have learned exactly as they have learned about the West—through study, reading, and conversation. On the other hand, they have *acquired* both African and Western culture simply by happening to be born when and where they were. They cannot really repudiate either one. They are in a netherworld between the two.

I am convinced that for all the lip service given to "Chaka instincts" and ancestral religious rites, the average intellectual doesn't really have his heart and soul in it. He can respect the old gods and rituals, but he cannot honestly believe in them. Magic and witchcraft retain a certain fascination for him, and still elicit a visceral response, but his head is committed to science. In his profounder reveries, he dreams of an eventual synthesis of African and Western cultures, but meanwhile he enjoys exercising his mind on existentialism, Toynbee, Freud, Jung, and Zen Buddhism. His life as husband, father, neighbor, student, or breadwinner is largely dictated by middle-class values and mores, with just about the same degree of faithfulness and rebellion as one finds in his Western counterpart. He has mixed feelings of admiration and scorn for those who seem to be "settled" and committed to an over-all authoritarian scheme of life, whether it be Moslem, Christian, Communist, chamber of commerce, or tribal animist.

Some of his fellow intellectuals give up on the tension of trying to balance African and Western values and take the leap into a "total" commitment, such as joining the Communist party or becoming all-out Christians or going whole-hog for an ancestral faith. But our "average" intellectual and an amazingly high percentage of his fellows cannot bring themselves to such a fateful decision. They cleave to the netherworld, sometimes complaining about their frustrations and high blood pressure, but more often reaffirming their proud intention to see the "new way" through.

Modernity, the West's spiritual legacy to Africa, has penetrated the heart, soul, and mind of the African elite. Yet when the African speaks from his heart, soul, and mind, he is generally anti-Western and frequently anti-Christian. His search for a self is tragically complicated, in part by his inward conflict of resentment toward the West, and in part by the outer reality that though the Western "oppressors" are gone or will soon be going, he cannot possibly advocate tossing out also the legacy of modernity. If he is to be other than a "black European," he must have something that *he* can contribute to the West. Thus his absorption with African arts, poetry, rhythms, and spirituality! But how many Westerners know of these African gifts? At best a handful. So there must be something else—some tremendous and unique quality—which Africa can hold up to the West for *all* Westerners to see. The elite as a group is certain that the "something" exists, but there is no real agreement as to what it is—no, not *la negritude*, or *muntu*, or even "African personality."

Let us be certain of this. We of the West cannot solve the African's spiritual problem for him. We cannot consummate his search for a self. Above all we must not stand shouting at him that he *has* to choose; choose our way or "backwardness," choose Christ or Communism, choose complete Westernization or go back to the jungle!

The Ghanaian poet Dei-Anang wrote:

> Here we stand——
> Poised between two civilizations
> Backward? to days of drums
> And festal dances in the shade
> Of sun-kist palms.
> Or forward?
> Forward!
> Toward?
> The slums, where man is dumped upon man? . . .
> The factory
> To grind hard hours
> In an inhuman mill
> In one long ceaseless spell?

The West has already done too much spread-eagling of the African between two, *and only two,* alternatives. He is not going to buy it. What he wants to become is a new man, who finds a way to a unique, creative remolding of his life, as a culture and as a person. How can he do it? *Can* he do it? And if he does, what will this new man really be like? No one can say—least of all the African himself. But that he has a right to try, this we can all say!

A Short but Choice Reading List

Changing Africa and the Christian Dynamic. The Center for the Study of the Christian World Mission. University of Chicago Press, 1960.

ACHEBE, CHINUA. *Things Fall Apart.* Heinemann, 1958.

AWOLOWO, CHIEF OBAFEMI. *Awo: The Autobiography of Chief Obafemi Awolowo.* Cambridge University Press, 1960.

BAETA, C. G. *Christianity and African Culture.*

BOLLINGEN SERIES 32. *African Folktales and Sculpture.* Pantheon Books.

CONTON, WILLLIAM. *The African.* New American Library, 1961.

DANQUAH, J. B. *The Akan Doctrine of God.* Lutterworth Press, 1944.

DELF, GEORGE. *Jomo Kenyatta.* Gollancz, 1961.

EVANS-PRITCHARD, EDWARD. *Witchcraft, Oracles and Magic Among the Azande.* Oxford University Press, 1937.

FIELD, M. J. *Religion and Medicine of the Ga People.* Oxford University Press, 1937.

FIELD, M. J. *Search For Security.* Faber and Faber, 1960.

GELFAND, MICHAEL. *Shona Ritual.* Juta, 1959.

GERDENER, G. B. A. *Recent Developments in the South African Mission Field.* N. G. Kerk-Uitgewers, 1958.

HERSKOVITS, MELVILLE J. *The Myth of the Negro Past.* Beacon Press, 1958.

ITALIAANDER, ROLF. *The New Leaders of Africa.* Prentice-Hall, Inc., 1961.

JAHN, JANHEINZ. *Muntu.* Grove Press, 1961.

KENYATTA, JOMO. *Facing Mount Kenya.* Secker and Warburg, 1938.

NKRUMAH, KWAME. *Ghana: the Autobiography of Kwame Nkrumah.* Thomas Nelson & Sons, 1957.

OLDHAM, J. H. *New Hope in Africa*. Longmans, Green.

PARRINDER, GEOFFREY. *Religion in an African City*. Oxford University Press, 1953.

PARRINDER, GEOFFREY. *African Traditional Religion*. Hutchinson's University Library, 1954.

PARRINDER, GEOFFREY. *Witchcraft*. Pelican Books, 1958.

PAUW, B. A. *Religion in a Tswana Chiefdom*. Oxford University Press, 1960.

ROSS, EMORY. *African Heritage*. Friendship Press, 1952.

RUTHERFORD, PEGGY, editor. *African Voices*. Grosset & Dunlap, 1961.

SACHS, WULF. *Black Anger*. Grove Press, 1947.

SITHOLE, NBABANINGI. *African Nationalism*. Oxford University Press, 1959.

SMYTHE, HUGH H. AND MABEL M. *The New Nigerian Elite*. Stanford University Press, 1961.

STACEY, TOM. *The Brothers M*. Pantheon, 1960.

SUNDKLER, B. G. M. *Bantu Prophets in South Africa*. Lutterworth Press, 1948.

SWANSON, GUY E. *The Birth of the Gods*. Michigan University Press, 1960.

TAYLOR, J. V. *Christianity and Politics in Africa*. Penguin Books, 1957.

TRIMMINGHAM, J. SPENCER. *Islam in West Africa*. Oxford University Press, 1959.

WELBOURN, F. B. *East African Rebels*. SCM Press, 1961.

WESTERMANN, DIEDRICH. *Africa and Christianity*. Oxford University Press, 1935.

WILLOUGHBY, W. C. *The Soul of the Bantu*. Doubleday, Doran & Co., 1928.

Index